Please return to Elaine Woodall →

HARRY PRIME

IAPC, Montclair State College
Upper Montclair, N.J. 07043
©1987 by Matthew Lipman. All rights reserved.
Published 1987
Printed in the United States of America

Chapter One

It probably wouldn't have happened if Harry hadn't fallen asleep in the TALE class that evening. (TALE stood for Thinking And Learning Environment.)

Well, he didn't really fall asleep either. His mind just wandered off. The teacher, Kevin Bradley—everyone called him Kevin—had been talking about the solar system. He'd been talking about how all the planets revolve around the sun, and Harry just stopped listening, because all at once he had this picture in his mind of the great, flaming sun and all the smaller planets revolving steadily around it.

- Suddenly Harry knew that Kevin was looking directly at him. Harry heard Kevin address him: "Harry Prime! Can you tell us what has a long tail and revolves around the sun once every 77 years?"

- Harry realized he had no idea of the answer Kevin expected. A long tail? For a moment he played with the idea of saying, "a dog star." (Harry remembered his daughter once reading to him from the *Child's Book of Knowledge* that the star named Sirius was called the "dog star.") But he wasn't sure that Kevin would find such an answer very funny.

  Kevin didn't have much of a sense of humor, but he was patient. Harry knew Kevin would wait a few seconds for Harry to figure something out.

- Harry could still hear Kevin saying, "All planets revolve about the sun." And this thing with a tail: it also goes around the sun. Could it also be a planet? It seemed worth a try. "A planet?" he asked, rather doubtfully.

- Harry wasn't prepared for the snickers from the class.

If he'd been paying attention, he would have heard Kevin say that the thing in question was Halley's comet. "Comets go around the sun just as planets do," Kevin had said, "but they definitely are *not* planets."

Fortunately the class was over at that point. But as Harry rode the subway home, he still felt badly about not having been able to answer Kevin correctly.

Also, he was puzzled. How had he gone wrong? He went back over the way he had tried to figure out the answer. "All planets revolve around the sun," Kevin had said, very distinctly. And this thing with the tail, it also revolves around the sun. Only it *isn't* a planet.

"Oh, wait a minute," Harry said to himself. "This means that some of the things that go around the sun aren't planets. Okay, so all planets revolve around the sun, but some things that aren't planets do too!"

And then Harry had an idea. "Look," he said to himself, "it's true that all *planets* are *things that revolve around the sun*. But it's false that all *things that revolve around the sun* are *planets*. So what's that mean? It means that a sentence can't be reversed! If you put the last part of a sentence first, it'll no longer be true. For example, take a sentence like, 'All oaks are trees.' If you turn it around, it becomes 'All trees are oaks.' But that's false!"

The example worked! Harry was excited. He decided to try a few more. First he thought of the sentence, "All cats are animals." When reversed, it became "All animals are cats." "Not true at all, no way!" Harry thought. He was delighted!

He tried another sentence: 'All Frenchmen are Europeans.'' But the reverse didn't follow at all. All Europeans are Frenchmen? Definitely not!

Harry was fascinated by his discovery. And he was thrilled when he began to think of what it might mean. For example, if he'd only known it earlier this evening, he might have avoided that awful embarrassment!

Just then he saw Lisa Torrey. Lisa was also in the TALE class, but Harry didn't know she took the same subway home each evening as he did. They found two seats together when some people got off at the next station.

They talked about what they were getting out of the class, and about Kevin. But Harry couldn't keep from telling Lisa what he'd been thinking about. "I've just had this funny idea," he said, "that when you turn sentences around, they're no longer true."

Lisa frowned as if to say, "What's so wonderful about that?"

"Look," said Harry, "give me a sentence, any sentence, and I'll show you."

Lisa continued to look doubtful. "But what *kind* of sentence? I can't just think up any sentence offhand. What would you like it to be about?"

"Well," said Harry, "a sentence with two kinds of things in it, like dogs and cats, or ice cream cones and food, or astronauts and people."

Lisa thought. Then just as she was about to say something, and Harry was awaiting impatiently for her to come out with it, she shook her head and thought some more.

- "Come on, two things, *any* two things," Harry begged.

  Finally Lisa made up her mind. "No eagles are lions," she announced.

- Harry pounced on the sentence the way his kids, Linda and Tyrone, would pounce on food when they were hungry. In an instant, Harry had the sentence reversed: "No lions are eagles." He was stunned. The first sentence, "No eagles are lions," had been true. But so

- was the sentence when reversed, for "No lions are eagles" was also true!

  Harry was perplexed. "It worked before! I don't understand why . . ." he started to say aloud, but he couldn't finish his sentence.

- Lisa looked at him wonderingly. "Why couldn't she have given me a sentence that worked?" Harry thought, with a flash of resentment. But then it occurred to him that, if he had really figured out a rule for all sentences, it should work on any sentence, even the one Lisa gave

- him. So it really wasn't her fault.

For the second time that evening, Harry felt that he had failed. His only comfort was that Lisa wasn't laughing at him. "I really thought I had something there," he said to her dejectedly. "I really thought I had it."

"You tried it out?" she asked. Her grey eyes, set wide apart, were clear and serious.

"Of course," Harry responded. "I took sentences like 'All trees are oaks,' and 'All cats are animals,' and 'All Frenchmen are Europeans,' and I found that when the last part was put first, the sentences were no longer true."

"But the sentence I gave you wasn't like yours," Lisa replied quickly. The subway car lurched and they were both jolted momentarily. Then Lisa went on, "Every one of your sentences began with the word 'all.' But my sentence began with the word 'no.' "

Lisa was right! But could that have made the difference? There was only one thing to do: try some more sentences that began with the word 'no.' Lisa stood up. "My station's coming up next," she said.

- Harry was desperately afraid she would get off without trying out her idea. "Look," he pleaded with her, "let's try it. What about 'No subway cars are kangaroos'?"
- Lisa grinned. "The reverse is also true: 'No kangaroos are subway cars.' And if it's true that 'No books are ballet dancers,' then it must be true that 'No ballet dancers are books.'" The train slid into the station, and she was gone before Harry could thank her.
- When he got home, he found his kids standing in front of the refrigerator. Harry tuned into the conversation. Linda was saying, "Y'know that Mrs. Bates from next door? Well every day, about the time I come home, I see her going into the liquor store. And y'know what?
- It makes me think about all those people who just can't stop drinking. I wonder if..."

Tyrone completed Linda's sentence: "You wonder if she's like them?"

- Linda nodded. Suddenly something in Harry's mind went "CLICK!" But he restrained himself.

"Linda," Tyrone said, with just a hint of exasperation in his voice, "just because, according to you, all people who can't stop drinking are people who go to the liquor store, that doesn't mean that all people who go to the liquor store are people who can't stop drinking."

"Well, all *right*!" Harry murmured softly, and Tyrone made believe he didn't know his father was pleased.

As for Harry, he sat down at the kitchen table, poured himself a beer, and stared at the foam converting itself into liquid. He felt happier than he had felt in days.

Chapter Two

The next evening, as Harry was about to enter the old brownstone in which the TALE classes were held, he met Tony Basilio. Tony was usually the first one to catch on to anything Kevin tried to teach the class. Also, he could figure out number problems in his head, without even writing them down. Harry couldn't help being a bit jealous of Tony.

Harry thought Tony might be interested in what he and Lisa had figured out the day before. He related their discovery that you could turn sentences that begin with 'no' around, but you can't turn them around if they begin with 'all.'

- Tony shrugged and said, "So what?"

"So what, what?" Harry replied.

- "I mean, first of all, I don't see the point of it. What good is it to know you can turn this sentence around and can't turn that one around? And secondly, how many sentences are there that begin with 'all' or 'no'? Very few. Thirdly, I'll bet I could come up with some exceptions to your rule if I thought about it for a while." With that, Tony went up the steps and into the building.

- But Harry lingered on the front steps. Tony's remarks bothered him. Maybe his "discovery" didn't amount to much after all.

Harry entered the classroom just as Kevin was about to explain how fractions work. As part of his explanation, Kevin remarked that there are all sorts of combinations that equal a single number. Harry could overhear Tony, sitting behind him, explaining to Tom Schultz, "It's easy. Look:

-         eight plus two equals ten
        five plus five equals ten

twelve minus two equals ten

twenty divided by two equals ten

five times two equals ten . . ."

After some hesitation, Tom said, "I have trouble with division." Middle-aged and heavy-set, Tom worked in a grocery store.

Tony answered impatiently, "You don't *have* to know how to divide. It's just a for instance. I'm just trying to show you how many different ways you can make the number ten. There must be thousands of ways, and they're all equal to ten."

The conversation between Tony and Tom lingered in Harry's mind. "If there are many ways of forming a number," he said to himself, "couldn't there be lots of different *words* all equal to the same word? Like my kids will call me 'dad,' or 'pop.' " Then he had an idea. Could it be that words like "all" and "no" are really like the number ten that Tony was explaining to Tim? Because if that were so, then all sorts of other sentences could be *changed* into sentences beginning with either

- the word "all" or the word "no."

Harry tried to figure out some other sentences that he could change around the way he wanted to. He couldn't think of a single one. His mind drifted off for a moment
- to his 11-year-old twins. He wondered what they were up to.

After a while, Harry began to wonder if the others in the class might be able to help him. He raised his hand and when Kevin called on him, Harry explained the pro-
- blem and asked if Kevin would allow the class to try to help. Kevin was known to be okay, and, as Harry expected, he agreed. He even stated the problem over again to the class because, in his excitement and frustration, Harry hadn't explained it very well.
- The first suggestion came from Rudy Garlock. "Look," Rudy said, "suppose I were talking about the people in this room. I could say, '*All* the people in this room are adults,' but I could also say, '*Each* person in this room is an adult,' or I could say, '*Every* person in
- this room is an adult,' and those three sentences all

mean the same thing. Because if we're all adults here, then each and everyone of us is an adult."

Kevin picked up a piece of chalk, went over to the blackboard and gravely wrote at the top, "Expressions that mean the same thing as 'ALL'." Then he began a list:

1. Each

2. Every

Lisa's hand shot up. "*Any,*" she announced, " 'cause if we're all adults here, then *any* one of us you choose will turn out to be an adult." Kevin turned back to the board and wrote, "3. Any."

Tony had his own hand up before Lisa had finished talking. "How about 'a'?" he asked. "I mean, if I say, 'A person in this room is sure to be an adult,' that's just the same as saying, 'All the people in this room are adults,' isn't it?"

As Kevin added "4. A" to his list, Harry wondered if he should object to Tony's suggestion. The sentence, "A person in this room is guilty," hovered in his mind, but he couldn't put into words his feeling that it was an exception to Tony's rule.

"It seems to me," said Kevin, after a moment had gone by without any new suggestions, "it doesn't have to be a particular word at all. It's the way the sentence is constructed. For example, suppose the first word in the sentence is the subject of the sentence itself. If I say, 'Potato chips are salty,' or if I say, 'Cadillacs are expensive,' I mean that *all* potato chips are salty, and *all* Cadillacs are expensive."

Hearing no objections, Kevin wrote on the board, "5. No modifier at all."

Tom Schultz slowly raised his hand. "Well," he began hesitantly, "sometimes when I say 'if' I mean 'all.' Like, when I say, '*If* you're a person in this room, *then* you're an adult."

Kevin had no sooner finished writing "6. If...then..." on the board than the hour was up. "Why don't you copy these down?" Kevin suggested, over the noise of chairs being pushed back and people making conversation.

Harry was grateful to Kevin for having stopped the regular lesson long enough to take up Harry's question. "Well, we did get *something* accomplished," Harry said to himself. "We showed Tony that even if only a few sentences actually do begin with the word 'all,' still there are lots and lots of others that can be changed to the 'all' form."

But Harry hadn't forgotten Tony's other question, "What good is any of this?" Nor could Harry think of a good answer. As he lingered on the sidewalk in front of the building, he saw Tony coming out, looking glum.

"Is something the matter?" Harry asked.

Tony looked as if he might just turn away, but then he shrugged and sat down on the steps. "My kid always talks as though, when he grows up, he won't study to be an engineer, which is what *I* wanted to be. When I tell him I want him to become an engineer, he gets mad at me."

"What makes you think he'd make a good engineer?" Harry asked.

"Well, he always gets good grades in math. So I say to him, 'All engineers are good in math, and you're good in math, so figure it out for yourself.'"

For a moment, Harry didn't reply. He was repeating Tony's words, turning them over in his mind. Then suddenly he exclaimed, "Tony! *It's not right!*"

"I know," Tony replied gloomily, "it sure ain't!"

"I mean," said Harry with a grin, "you said, 'All engineers are good in math,' right? But that's one of those sentences that can't be turned around! So it *doesn't* follow that 'All people who're good in math are engineers.' And you know that's so. There are lots of doctors who're good in math, and airplane pilots who're good in math, and all sorts of other people who aren't engineers who are good in math. So just because you're good in math, it doesn't follow that you have to become an engineer!"

Tony said, "So the kid was right when he said he couldn't follow my reasoning! Now I see it plain as day: even if it's true that *all* engineers are good in math, it doesn't follow that *only* engineers are good in math." •

With that, Tony got on the bus that had pulled up to the curb, and Harry headed for the subway.

Chapter Three

Lisa, Fran Woodson and Jill Panikkos worked together in the same factory, took their lunches together at the same deli, and attended the same class two evenings a week at the TALE center. As the weather was pleasant, they sat outside on a bench to eat their lunch and sit in the sun.

Lisa said, "When I was a kid, I used to make peanut butter and jelly sandwiches, and you should have seen my father's face! He used to say that even the *thought* of that sort of junk made him ill!"

"I know," replied Jill. "My mother always used to

tell me I should drink milk instead of taking a can of grape soda to school. Milk. Ugh!"

But Lisa was still thinking about her father's remark. "The thought of peanut butter and jelly made him sick? How could just a thought do that?"

"My thoughts often make me happy," Jill said, after a moment. "Like, when I'm on the assembly-line, I'll think of our dog, Sandy. He's a young collie. He's always jumping up on people, and my husband calls him Romeo. Before I go to work each morning, I walk him, and he urinates on everything that even *looks* like a tree!"

"I know what you mean," Lisa said, bringing Jill back to the point. "When you're away from home you think about him, and somehow it's a nice warm feeling to keep a thought that you like in mind."

Jill was pleased that Lisa understood. "That's right," she said, "when I leave Sandy in the morning, I take the thought of him to work with me. Right now it's almost as though I can feel it jump up on my lap to be patted!"

Lisa studied a green pear that was her dessert. "Isn't it funny," she remarked, "our talking about thoughts. You know, Harry Prime's always talking about how we think. Remember that discussion we had in class the other day?"

"How we think?" repeated Fran, who had made no comment until that point.

Lisa said, "Yes, Harry's always talking about thinking."

"Well, why not?" asked Jill. "We talk about everything else—like wars and drug addicts and garbage collection . . ."

Fran wasn't ready to let the topic drop. "When you say 'thinking'," she asked, "what do you mean—the thoughts we have in our minds—you know, ideas and memories and dreams and stuff like that—or the *way* we think?"

Jill answered Fran's question with another question: "What do you mean, the *way* we think?"

"Well," said Lisa, "one way of thinking is, like,

- figuring things out. When you already know something and you want to go beyond what you already know, that's what you do: figure things out."

- "But just having thoughts is different from really thinking," Fran commented. "My mind's always full of thoughts, but I have no idea where they come from. They just bubble up out of nowhere like the bubbles in this can of soda."

- Jill said softly, "Gee, I don't know; I don't think of my thoughts like that. To me they're something like bats hanging asleep upside down in a dark cave. At night they wake up and they beat around inside the cave making an awful lot of noise, and I can't sleep for all the thoughts that run through my mind. Yet every now and

- then one gets out of the cave and then he's changed into a bird—even an eagle, maybe—he's free and away, and there's no holding him, and he can go way, way off, as far away as he wants."

- Lisa nodded. "My mind, why it's like a world of its own. It's like my room in my house. I have things on my desk or on my bookshelves—rocks and books and photographs, things like that—and sometimes I pick one up and look at it and sometimes another. And I do the same with my thoughts. I have my favorite thoughts. And I have others I don't want to even think about.''

"But thoughts aren't *really* real," Jill remarked. "I mean, they're not real like the things in your room. My *thought* of my dog isn't a real dog. The real Sandy is all full of fur, but my thought of him isn't furry at all!"

"Well, but it's still a real thought," Fran answered.

"Do you mean," Lisa asked Jill, "that if there's something out there that your thought is like, then your thought is just a *copy* or *imitation,* and isn't really real? For example, if there's a dog out there named Sandy, then the thought of the dog isn't really real, because it's just a *copy* of the dog? But there are lots of thoughts I have that aren't copies of anything!"

"Like what?" Jill demanded.

"Like, say, numbers," Lisa responded triumphantly. "Did you ever see a number walking down the street, or

- standing around anywhere? The only place numbers are real is in your mind. And I'll bet there are lots of other things like numbers that are real only in your mind."

- "That's right," Fran chimed in. "How about feelings? When I feel sad or happy, aren't those feelings only in my mind? I never saw a feeling walking down the street, either!"

- Lisa didn't reply. She wasn't sure about feelings. Or at least she wasn't sure just where they were. But she knew she had a mind that was rich in colors and tastes and sounds that she could remember, as well as in ideas that she thought up, or that just popped into her head. She decided it might be something to talk to Harry Prime about sometime.

- The conversation moved on to other subjects, including talking about things that had happened to them long ago, when the three of them had been kids in school. Fran told one story with evident relish. It seems she had been standing in the hall and the bell for class was about

- to ring. Two monitors were standing at the door. Both

boys were large and rather heavy, and they decided to tease Fran by not giving her much room to pass. Maybe they thought they did it because she was a girl, and she thought they did it because she was a girl and Black too, but she didn't care for that kind of teasing, so she pushed them out of her way. The teacher turned around just in time to see what Fran had done, and she spoke to Fran very sharply about it.

Fran said nothing. Then she did something that no one expected her to do. She got up on the first desk in the front row, and she began to leap from one desk to the next until she had circled the room. Then she sat down quietly at her seat.

Long afterwards—for the rest of the day in fact—Lisa had in her mind this strange picture of Fran as a child, leaping proudly and gracefully from desk to desk in the silent classroom. It was an image that came back to her mind very vividly as she sat on the park bench, her eyes closed against the sun. But then another image crossed her mind. It was the factory floor, and lots of animals were gathered around the water fountain. They weren't doing much: some were drinking but most of them were just sitting or standing there. And then Lisa noticed something odd about each of them. The zebras had cat-like claws. The giraffes had long, furry, cat-like tails. The elephants had huge, cat-like whiskers. A buffalo was trying to flatten itself on the floor, preparing to spring like a cat upon a green-eyed field mouse. The chimpanzees all had pointed ears and slanted eyes, and a grizzly bear kept licking his paw, then washing his face with it, just the way a cat does. Such a peculiar scene! Lisa wondered if she were dreaming.

And then, oddly, she remembered something she had been talking about with Harry. "All cats are animals," they had agreed, but you can't turn the sentence around and say, "Therefore, all animals are cats."

"So all animals aren't cats," Lisa thought to herself, "but in imagination they can be! And in dreams, too. I can imagine what I please, and when I do, Harry's rule won't apply!"

It was something that had been troubling her and now she had worked it out. She felt satisfied, and with a little smile she allowed herself to drift off into another daydream of the water fountain on the factory floor where all animals were cats. She pictured too a farm where all the vegetables were onions, even the cucumbers and the tomatoes. And she even thought of a world where everyone was thirty years old—even the babies and the grownups, even her grandfather and grandmother—everyone. And yet, all the while she was daydreaming, she knew that when she finished, it would be to a world where all thirty-year-olds are people but not all people are thirty-year-olds—and to a world where all cats are animals, but not all animals are cats.

* * *

But Tony Basilio tossed about on his bed that night and couldn't fall asleep. Tony enjoyed doing math problems, but he also liked English, maybe because it wasn't his native language and he was discovering its

- grammar for the first time. Tony was fascinated by the ways in which the parts of sentences fitted together. "You can take a sentence apart just like when you take apart an old alarm clock and spread all the pieces out on
- the floor in front of you," he once said to Tom Schultz. Tom was always asking Tony for help with his arithmetic or his English.

  What Tony was thinking about now was Harry's discovery, and what had happened when he tried it out
- on his son, Peter. "Peter," Tony had said, "remember what I told you the other day, that all engineers are good in math, and that's why you ought to be an engineer?"

  Peter squinted at his father, as if to say, "Yes, what
- about it?"

  "Well," said Tony, pushing up his glasses which had settled down on his nose, "you said you couldn't follow my reasoning, didn't you?"

  Peter nodded. He obviously wondered what his father
- was getting at.

"Look," Tony said briskly, "take that sentence, 'All engineers are people who are good in math. Well now, it just doesn't follow from that sentence that 'All people who are good in math are engineers.''

Peter no longer look mystified. "I get it! You mean, if you turn the sentence around, it'll no longer be true!"

Tony permitted himself a little smile. "Yes—and so what follows from that?"

Peter grinned triumphantly. "I don't know what follows, but I know what *doesn't* follow! Just because I'm good in math, it *doesn't* follow that I have to become an engineer." A frown crossed his face. "Hey, I know it doesn't follow, but I don't quite know why."

"I don't know why either, but I'm willing to find out," said Tony. He took an old envelope out of his pocket and began to write on the back of it. "I'm going to draw a big circle, and I'm going to put a label on it, like this:

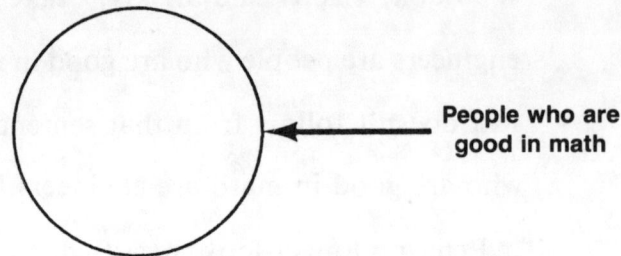

- What I mean is that all the people who are good in math are inside that circle, just like it was a big round fence or corral. Now I'm going to draw a second circle inside the first one, like this:

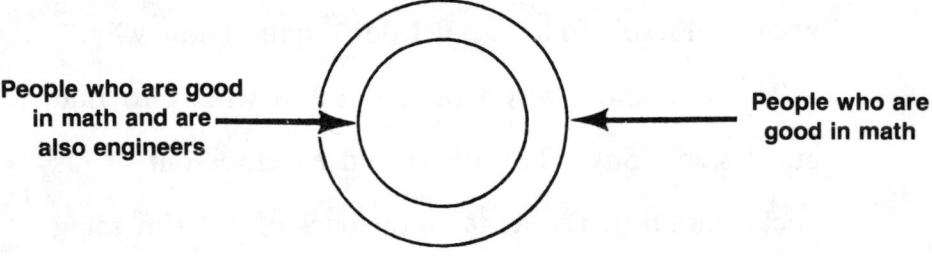

- This means that the smaller corral fences in only engineers, but all of them are good in math so they also are found within the larger corral. Now don't you see,

Peter, the smaller corral fits inside the larger one, but the larger one won't fit inside the smaller one?"

Peter stared at his father. "You mean, that's the reason we can't turn sentences around? Because a small group of people or things can be part of a larger group of people or things, but a larger group can't be part of a smaller group?"

"That's how it seems to work with sentences that begin with 'all,' " said Tony.

Peter slapped his hand on the table. "Oh, boy! Gee, wow! I can see it so clearly! It's like if you say, 'All cities in Texas are American cities,' it sure doesn't mean that 'All American cities are cities in Texas.' Texas is just *part* of America, so there's no way America can be just part of Texas."

Even though he was pleased with Peter's enthusiasm, Tony remained silent, thoughtfully massaging his chin. Then he spoke up again. "Y'know, Peter, it maybe doesn't follow for another reason. I mean, what I said was, 'All engineers *are* good in math. You're good in

- math. So you *ought to be* an engineer.' But can you really get an 'ought to be' from an 'are'? I kind of doubt it.''

- Peter would gladly have continued the conversation, but his father merely turned on the television set, and in a minute was completely lost in the evening news.

Chapter Four

Lisa did tell Harry Prime about her talk with Fran and Jill. "Fran says her thoughts are real," she told him.

"That's funny," Harry replied. "Just the other day, Suki Chen told me that when her brother was drawing—he's two years old—she heard him say, 'I have a think and I draw a line around my think!'"

"Well, are thoughts real or aren't they?" Lisa demanded.

"I'm not sure," Harry answered, staring at the THINKING AND LEARNING ENVIRONMENT sign in front of the Center. "In some ways, thoughts are even *more* real than things. Things come and go, depending on whether we're looking at them or not, but our thoughts we always carry with us. I can close my eyes and make the world disappear, but I can't close my mind and make my thoughts disappear."

Lisa shrugged and went inside, leaving Harry sitting on the steps. "Why did I get here so early?" she asked herself. "There's nothing to do!"

To her surprise, she found Kevin in the classroom, seated at his desk, which was a small mountain of papers and books. Kevin had been staring moodily out the window, but now he acknowledged Lisa's presence with a nod. "Lisa," he asked, "I wonder if I could ask you to help me. I'm trying to think of a topic for the weekend writing assignment, but I'm not happy with any of the ideas I've had."

"Like what?" Lisa wanted to know.

"Well, what would the class think of the topic, 'The Greatest Thing in the World'?"

Lisa stuck her lower lip out, reflected for a moment, and then said, "Not too good."

"Why?" asked Kevin.

"Well," Lisa said, "I doubt that anyone will find it very exciting. Anyhow, what do you mean, 'greatest'? Biggest? Or the most important?"

Kevin looked puzzled momentarily. Then he exclaimed. "Oh, you're right! It could mean both things, couldn't it? Well, how would you suggest I say it?"

"Why don't you just ask us to write about whatever interests us most?" Lisa responded.

Kevin nodded. Later, when the class was seated, he announced the topic as "The Most Interesting Thing In The World."

Tom Schultz put his hand up. "Do you mean, when you say 'thing,' some kind of educational subject, like history or biology, or do you just mean any kind of thing you can touch and pick up, like a baseball bat or a tennis racket?"

"Uh-uh, I've done it again!" said Kevin, looking

directly at Lisa. "You're quite right, Tom. I'll have to try to be more precise. Yes, the word 'thing' can have several meanings in the topic I gave you. It could be an object, like a tennis racket, something you can see and touch and measure, or it can be something rather vague and hard to define, like an activity."

"Doing your thing—that's an activity," commented Fran.

"Well," Kevin said, with a glance in Fran's direction, "I was thinking more of activities or processes—like breathing or rusting or flying or surfing—things like that."

Harry carefully jotted down the assignment, but it was Sunday before he tried writing anything. As usual, he wrote very slowly. And try as he might, he couldn't make the written words stay on the lines. His theme began this way:

THINKING

To me, the most interesting thing in the whole world is thinking. I know that lots of other things are also very important and wonderful, like electricity and magnetism and gravitation. But although we understand them, they can't understand us. So thinking must be something very special.

Harry wrote several more paragraphs, then put his paper in his briefcase. As he did so, a thought struck him. "There are lots of different subjects that we have to think about. But who ever heard of thinking about thinking?" He got his paper out and added, "If we think about electricity, we can understand *it* better, but when we think about thinking, we seem to understand ourselves better."

* * *

Linda and Tyrone finished up the dishes and sat down with Harry at the kitchen table. They talked about some of their experiences in class, and Harry told them

- about how Kevin had taken time out to discuss Harry's idea about turning sentences around, and how the others in the class had joined in to try to make basic sentences that worked like lowest common denominators.
- Harry didn't mention anything about how Ben Beck and Sam da Silva had teased him about his "simple language," as they called it. Harry didn't much like to be teased.

  Linda listened carefully. She always looked a little
- anxious, even when she wasn't. "Dad," she said, "it sounds good. But do you really think you can take all different kinds of sentences and reduce them to just two kinds, ones beginning with 'all,' and ones beginning with 'no'?"
- Harry said sure, but he really didn't feel very sure. Then he said, rather uncertainly, "Is it a question of *reducing* them to those two kinds, or of *translating* them into those two kinds?"

  Linda could make no reply. She found herself looking
- around the room—at the fish in the aquarium, at the

geraniums in the window, at the cookbooks on the shelves. Then she said, "How would you say something like, 'Seven chairs are in the room,' in your language?"

Harry knew, even before he tried the sentence, that it wasn't going to work. It wouldn't do to say, "*All* chairs are in the room," if there were just seven of them. And it surely wouldn't do to say that *no* chairs were in the room. Linda and Tyrone tried to help him, but it was no use. Besides, there were other sentences that came to mind just as difficult to figure out. What could anyone do with "Some chairs are in the room," or "Lots of chairs are in the room," or even something fantastic like, "Almost all the chairs ever made are in the room?"

In class the next day, Harry asked Kevin if he had any suggestions. "Well, Harry," Kevin said, "as I understand what you're trying to do, you want to substitute the word 'all' for a number of other words. Okay, but now you tell me that you don't know what to do with sentences that begin with words like 'almost all' and 'lots of' and 'a few' and so on. But are you sure there isn't one single word that could be substituted for any of these?"

Harry groaned, "I can't think of any."

"I can," someone said. Harry turned around. It was Mike Morawski, who'd been sitting behind him, listening to the conversation. "What you're looking for is a word that covers everything between 'all' and 'no.' So why not use 'some'?"

Harry's first impulse was to say, "Naaah, Mike, that'll never work!" But the more he thought of it, the more he thought Mike might just possibly be right. As Mike had said, a word was needed that would apply to every case that was less than *all* and more than *none*. So why not "some," just as Mike had suggested?

By the time Kevin had commented, "Sounds okay to me, Mike," Harry had made up his mind.

When it was time for math, Kevin told the class he would take a few moments out to make an addition to the basic language they were developing. And he told them about Mike Morawski's suggestion. The members of the class entered in their notebooks, "When less than *all* and more than *none,* say 'some'."

Kevin observed quietly, "I guess you could say it's a rule of substitution."

But Lisa, remembering her last conversation with Harry, said to herself, "It's a rule for substituting words, but as far as whole sentences go, it's a rule of *translation.*"

Now Tony Basilio had his hand up. "I see a problem."

"He *always* sees problems," Harry grumbled, half to himself.

"Look," said Tony, "when you were working with 'all' and 'no,' you sort of had like opposites of one another, y'know what I mean? I mean, 'all' is kind of like the opposite of 'no,' and 'no' is like the opposite of 'all.' But if you begin with just 'some,' you don't have anything opposite it!"

"But do we need it?" Harry demanded.

"Yes," Tony snapped, "because there are sentences I could show you."

- "Okay, show us," Harry replied. "Give us an example!" Even as he said it, he knew that Tony would.

  "Take a sentence like 'Most people aren't poor—' " Tony began.

- "That's wrong," said Darrel Thompson. "Most people aren't rich."

  Tony looked annoyed. "It's just a 'for instance,' " he said. "But okay, take another example: 'Lots of people don't like taking baths.' "

- "Well, *that's* true," said Anne Torbrandtson.

  Suddenly Harry saw the problem clearly. "The 'some' is okay!" he almost shouted. "The 'some' is okay! It's the *verbs* that change!" The class looked at him blankly. "In one case you have the verb 'are,' and
- in the other case you have the verb 'are not.' "

  Kevin looked at Tony. "Your point's a good one, Tony. A very good one. But Harry's right, too, I think. Let me see if I can summarize what we now have." He went to the blackboard. "I'll write four different
- sentences, but each having the same subject and

—44—

predicate, like this:

All courses are interesting.

No courses are interesting.

Some courses *are* interesting.

Some courses *are not* interesting.

Harry breathed a sigh of relief. What progress they had made!

Later that evening, Kevin returned Harry's paper on thinking. Kevin had written a good deal in the margins, but one sentence interested Harry particularly. "You're right, Harry," Kevin wrote. "There's no fact in the world that's more wonderful than our understanding of that fact!"

Harry read it over and over, with great admiration. "He put it so well," he thought. "I wish I could have said it so well." Then he shrugged.

He was the last to leave. Some were already on their way to the subway, some were waiting at the bus stop, and a number had begun to head towards the parking lot. As Harry prepared to cross the street in the direc-

- tion of the subway station, a car whizzed by and Harry quickly scrambled back onto the sidewalk. Although he didn't get a good look at either the car or the driver, his first thought was that the driver had been Tony.

Chapter Five

"Cops!" Mark Wallenda exclaimed when he came out of class the next evening and found a ticket on his car for being double-parked.

His cousin, Maria, who was also attending the TALE course, was as usual undisturbed. "That's just their job," she commented. "When you have a job to do, you say and do things you may not mean, like when you have a part in a play in school and you have to say lines you don't mean."

Mark said nothing. Maria was always explaining things to him. He usually disagreed with her, but he seldom knew why.

- Harry Prime came over, eating some candy-covered chocolates. He offered some to Mark and then, almost as an afterthought, offered some to Maria. They munched away in silence. A bit later, they drifted over to
- Gerties, a tiny coffeehouse half a block from the TALE center.

Sipping his coffee, Mark continued to scowl. "That course we're taking is for the birds!" he grumbled. "I'm bored to death in there."

- "I sort of like it," Harry said.

"Me too," Maria added. "Mark, how do you think you'll ever get your High School Equivalency Certificate if you don't take this course and pass it? And you've told me yourself, no certificate, no promotion:
- it's as simple as that! Just look at Harry: he's in much worse shape than you are. He's got two kids to take care of, and *he's* not complaining!"

Harry flushed and tried to change the subject by remarking, "Things aren't often all of one kind or all of
- another, y'know what I mean? I mean, like, when I was

in grammar school, some courses were good and some weren't." Suddenly there popped in Harry's mind the picture of Kevin writing on the blackboard:

Some courses *are* interesting.

Some courses *are not* interesting.

"I don't remember even one being good," said Mark. "They were *all* bad!"

"Mark," said Maria, with a faint note of annoyance in her voice, "just because you happened to find some courses boring, that doesn't mean they were *all* boring."

"It doesn't *mean* it," Mark muttered, "They just *were.*"

"In fact," Maria continued, as if she hadn't heard Mark's comment, "if some courses are boring, then it *must* be that there are other courses that *are not* boring."

Harry looked doubtfully at Maria. "What was that again?" he finally asked.

"I *said,*" Maria began, and she repeated her remark.

—49—

- "Go figure it out for yourself." She stared at Mark as he went to get himself another cup of coffee.

"It doesn't follow, Maria," Harry objected. "Look," he said, taking the almost-full bag of candies
- from his pocket, "suppose you didn't know what kind of candy was in this bag. And then you saw me take out three pieces of candy and they were all brown. Would it follow that there were other pieces still in the bag that weren't brown?"

- Maria answered, "You mean, would I know what color the others were without seeing them? No, I guess I wouldn't."

"That's *right!*" Harry exclaimed. "If all you know is that *some* of the candies in the bag are brown you can't
- say what color they *all* are, and you certainly can't say, because some of them *are* brown, that some must *not* be!"

Maria complained she didn't know what Harry was talking about *at all,* but by that time Mark had return-
- ed. "Maria," he said, "suppose a couple of Martians

—50—

were to walk into this coffeehouse here right now, and we saw they didn't have purple eyes. What would it mean about whatever other Martians there might be?"

Before Maria had a chance to reply, Harry burst in: "It wouldn't follow that the others *had* purple eyes, and it wouldn't follow that they *didn't* have purple eyes. You just wouldn't be able to tell, one way or another."

Maria looked thoughtful. "You're right, but people do think that way, just the same. They're always jumping to conclusions. If people meet one Polish person, or one Jewish or one Black person, right away they jump to the conclusion that this is the way *all* Polish people are, or all Black people, or all Jewish people."

"Jumping at conclusions is the only exercise some people get," said Harry.

"Or jumping on other people," commented Maria.

Harry would have liked to continue the conversation about the likelihood of purple-eyed Martians, but a thought troubled him: if a teacher says to a class, "Some of you didn't pass the test," doesn't it follow

- that the rest of them did?

However, Mark interrupted Harry's train of thought by saying, "All the courses in my school were awful. It was an awful school."

- "Were there better ones?" asked Harry.

"No," Mark replied, "there weren't then and there aren't now. Some kids in our neighborhood go to private school and some go to parochial school, and from what they tell me, the schools are awful
- everywhere."

"What makes them so bad?" Harry wanted to know.

Mark responded immediately. "Teachers! Principals! Boards of Education! They run the schools to suit themselves. As long as you do what you're told, you're okay.
- But if you don't, you're dead!"

"Mark!" exclaimed Maria. "They're *only* trying to do what's *good* for us!"

"Yeah," said Mark, "and you can be sure they'll *call* it good, no matter what they do."

- "Well," remarked Maria, "*someone* has to teach and

someone has to run the schools, so it has to be the trained professionals, because they *know* more than anyone else. It's the same way with other things. You wouldn't want to fly on an airplane where the pilot was on his first flight, would you? You wouldn't want to go to a hospital for an appendicitis operation where the surgeons and nurses were just orderlies and patients, would you? So what else is there to do but let professionals run the schools, since they're the only ones who can do it right?"

Mark looked glum. "I don't know. Maybe, if students ran the schools, things wouldn't be any worse than they are now. I don't see how they *could* be worse!"

Harry shook his head. "It's not a question of whether the schools should be run by students or by professional administrators. That's not the question at all. The real question is whether the schools should be run by people who know what they're doing or by people who don't know what they're doing."

- "What do you mean, 'know what they're doing'?" Maria asked.

  Harry shrugged. "Understand, I guess. Whoever runs the schools should understand students. I think Mark's
- right. Lots of times they don't. But the most important thing they need to understand is why students are in school in the first place."

  "They're in school to learn," Maria said.

  "Are they?" Harry asked. "What are they supposed
- to learn?"

  "Answers, I suppose." Maria wondered what Harry was driving at. Then she thought she caught on. "No, no, I take that back. They're supposed to be learning how to solve problems."
- Mark stared at Maria. "Should they be learning how to solve problems," he said finally with an air of wondering, "or should they be learning how to ask questions?"

  Harry thought he had the answer: "They should be
- learning how to think."

"Maybe they already think," was Mark's response, "but they never learn to think for themselves. No one wants to admit that we have minds of our own. People are always trying to fill our minds with all sorts of junk, but our minds are not a junkyard. It makes me so mad!"

"Well, what kind of school would you like your kids to go to?" Harry asked.

Mark studied his coffee cup at length, then replied, "What kind of school would I like them to go to? I'll tell you what kind of school. You wouldn't have to go to class unless you wanted to, and they'd have to make the courses real interesting in order to get you to attend. What's more, all the sciences courses would be taught like science fiction . . ."

"The trouble with what you're saying," Harry interrupted, "is that a lot of stuff that people are taught in school just can't be made interesting."

"Sure it can," replied Mark. "Look how they make stuff interesting in TV commercials. Lots of commercials are really great, yet all they're advertising is a lousy bar of soap!"

Harry grinned. "But that's all phony, Mark, and you know it."

"Sure," said Mark, "you're right. But the advertisers take something unimportant and jazz it up and make it seem glamorous, while in school they take subjects like history that are really very interesting, and they teach it in such a way as to make it seem boring and dull."

Harry shook his head. All he could say was, "I don't know, Mark. I just don't know if things could be made any better." But as he paid for his coffee, he couldn't help wondering if Mark might possibly be right.

* * *

On Sunday, Harry and his kids took a walk in the park that was a few blocks from where they lived. It was getting to be late in the afternoon, time to be leaving for home. But they lingered, lying on a grassy slope, chewing clover and wild onion, and looking up at the sky.

The sky was clear and blue, except for a huge white cloud that was moving slowly overhead. Suddenly, Tyrone exclaimed, "Look Linda—it's North America!"

And so it was. There was Alaska, and Hudson's Bay, and Florida, and the Gulf of Mexico. Only, California and Mexico seemed rather blurred. The three of them watched fascinated as the enormous continent swept past into the blue Pacific.

"That was great!" Linda exclaimed, when the cloud had become just a blur in the distance.

"Yeah, right," Tyrone replied. "But you know, it was *our idea.*"

"Whadd'ya mean, our idea?" Linda wanted to know.

"I mean," said Tyrone, "it was a wonderful cloud. But also, when you come to think of it, it was pretty wonderful for us just to lie here and be able to see it as North America sailing across the Pacific. You gotta admit that part of it, too."

Something crossed Harry's mind, the way a news

- flash comes on across the bottom of a TV screen. It was Kevin's comment: "No matter how wonderful something in the world may be, *understanding* how it works is something just as wonderful." It wasn't quite the way
- he'd put it, but it was pretty much the same idea.

  Harry heard Linda say, "I guess you don't have to fly to the moon or travel under the ocean in order to have adventures or see wonderful things. Sometimes they're right there in front of you for you to see."
- And he heard Tyrone reply, "Sometimes I get real excited by my own ideas, and I pace up and down in my room, or I punch my punching bag, or I do all sorts of crazy things until I calm down."

  But Harry's thoughts turned to the conversation he'd
- had with Mark as they had walked out of the coffee shop. "Do you think someone purposely tried to give me a scare the other night?" Harry had asked, and he related how the car had brushed him back from the curb.
- "I'm not sure," said Mark slowly. "But I was the

first one out of class that night, and I remember seeing this new guy, Ben Beck, muttering to himself about how the cops kept ticketing his car. He does look kind of weird. Maybe it was him."

"Ben Beck! But why should *he* want to give me a hard time?" Harry thought. "What's he got against *me?*"

As they walked home, Harry insisted that Linda and Tyrone not get too close to the curb. Anybody crazy enough to try something like that once might be crazy enough to try it a second time. And the next time, it might not be just a near miss.

Chapter Six

"There's a tune just keeps going through my head," said Jill Panikkos. "We have it on a cassette and my kid brother keeps playing it. It's called 'The Saucer's Appendage,' or something like that."

Fran corrected Jill with a grin: "*The Sorcerer's Apprentice.*"

Jill laughed at her own mistake: "Anyhow," she went on, "it's like I'm *haunted* by that tune. It comes to me at work and when I'm trying to sleep and all other sorts of times. I wish I could just shake my head and make it go away."

It was Friday night, and Fran Wood and Laura O'Reilly were visiting with Jill. Jill lived close by the TALE center, and since she, Fran and Laura never seemed to have enough time to chat before the evening sessions, they had begun to make the Panikkos apartment their once-a-week gathering place for continuing the conversations that had begun in the classroom.

"Sometimes I have *dreams* like that," said Laura. "My grandmother was sick a long time, and then when she died, I kept dreaming about her, and I always had the feeling that she was *making* me dream about her. Yet how could that be when she was dead already?"

"Dead people can't do anything to you," said Fran, who then said, "at least, I don't think they can."

Jill looked at Fran questioningly. "It's funny," she said. "The last time I listened to that cassette was a week ago, but I've been hearing the music in my mind ever since. It made a strong impression on me. So isn't it possible that Laura's grandmother's death simply made a strong impression on *Laura,* and that's why she's been dreaming of it ever since?"

Laura shook her head. "When I see the moon, it's because the moon is out there, making me see it, right? And in my mind just now I heard your voice because you were speaking to me. So I think that all the thoughts that are *in* my mind are caused by things that are *outside* my mind."

"That's ridiculous," said Jill. "There are all sorts of imaginary things that are only *in* your mind, and there's nothing like them outside at all."

"Like what?" Laura asked.

"Like—well—the creatures from outer space in horror movies," Jill replied.

"Okay," said Laura, "but even with those imaginary creatures, there are real people who make them up and tell us about them or make movies about them and in that way make us think of them . . ."

"Laura," Fran interrupted, "you keep talking about what's *in* your mind and what's *not* in your mind. But what's a 'mind'? And how do you know you have one?"

- Laura, relaxed on the sofa, yawned and stretched and somehow managed to wiggle her toes at the same time. "I know I've got a mind," she replied, "just like I know I've got a body."

- It was at this point that Jill's husband, who worked an evening shift, came home. Jill introduced him to Laura and Fran, but he did not stay to talk. Before long the earlier conversation was resumed on the same topic.

- Fran insisted that a person could see and touch his body, but he couldn't see or touch his mind. "When you say 'mind,' " Fran concluded, "all you're talking about is your brain. Only things you can see or touch are real."

- "Lots of real things are things we can't see or touch," Laura objected. "For example, if I go for a swim, is there really some kind of thing called 'a swim'? If I go for a walk or a ride, are there really things called 'walks' or 'rides'?"

"So what are you saying?" Fran demanded.

- "What I think Laura's saying," said Jill, "is that

what we call thinking is something we do, like swimming or walking are things we do."

"That's right," Laura agreed, "that's just what I mean. When I said before I had a mind, I meant that I *mind* things. I mind the telephone, or my little nephew, or I just mind my own business. Having a mind is nothing but minding."

But Fran wasn't happy with the solution Jill and Laura had arrived at. "I agree," she said, "maybe the mind isn't quite the same thing as the brain. I know I said before it was, but I've changed my mind." Everyone laughed, then Fran went on. "What I mean is, you can't see electricity, but it's real. So why couldn't our thoughts be something electrical in the brain?"

Jill's husband appeared in the doorway. "Anyone thirsty?" he inquired amiably. "A drink? Beer? Coffee?" Laura, Jill and Fran each asked for a diet drink, and Jill's husband had them ready in an instant.

"Ralph," said Jill, "what do *you* think a mind is?"

Ralph looked at Jill warily. "A long time ago, I used

to think the mind was some kind of thin, smoky stuff, like one's breath—"

"Did you think you could see it in cold weather, the way you can see your breath in cold weather?" Jill interrupted.

"No," her husband replied. "I simply thought of it as something real but invisible. You couldn't ever see it, but it was where your thoughts were, and your feelings, and your memories and imaginings, and they too were all made of this same thin, filmy substance."

"Oh!" Jill exclaimed, "that's so right! That's exactly what the mind is!"

Ralph slowly cleaned his glasses. "Maybe."

"Well, what else *could* it be?" Jill demanded.

Ralph put his arm around Jill's shoulders. "I really don't know," he said, resting his feet on the coffee table. "Sometimes I think it's nothing but language."

"Language?" Jill asked.

"Well, I've noticed that when children first begin to talk, they talk to other people," said Ralph. "When other people aren't around to talk to, the children keep right on talking as if they were. In other words, they start talking to themselves. And they talk to themselves more and more quietly until they don't make any sounds at all. Perhaps that's what's called thinking."

"And you mean," said Fran, "that at first children would see things only when those things were present, but when those things weren't present, the children would hold on to them by remembering or imagining them? So the thoughts in our minds are really just the traces of things in our memories?"

"Hey, Fran, what do *I* know?" Ralph replied. "I never thought of it quite like that."

Just then, Mr. Panikkos, Jill's father-in-law, came in, sipping a cup of tea. "I could hear your conversation from the kitchen," he remarked. "What's it all about?"

Jill said, "We were trying to figure out what we mean when we talk about a person's mind."

"I think I know what it is!" Laura exclaimed. "It's what people have and animals don't have!"

- Mr. Panikkos found a chair and sat down rather heavily. "No, no, that won't do!" he said, looking quite troubled. "The difference is not between men and animals. Not at all. Man is also an animal. The dif-
- ference is that man is an animal with a *culture,* and that's the reason we believe he has a mind. In fact, *any* animal has a mind to the extent that it has a culture."

"What in the world is he talking about?" Laura wondered. "He sounds just like a book!"

- But Jill wasn't afraid to challenge her father-in-law. "Dad," she said, "you once said that any creature with a heart was also a creature with a liver. Now even if that's true, it wouldn't follow that hearts are livers."

Laura laughed, "If a person needed a heart
- transplant, it wouldn't do to give him someone else's liver!"

"Still," said Fran to Mr. Panikkos, "you made it sound as if the mind and ~~the brain~~ *culture* are one and the same thing, just because they're always found together. But
- that doesn't *have* to be so, does it?"

Mr Panikkos ran his fingers through his sparse, white hair and looked at Fran sadly but tolerantly. "I'll try to explain it to you some other time," he said gently, and with that, he and Ralph went off to watch TV.

Mr. Laliberte ran his fingers through his sparse, white hair and looked sad. "I can still hear him, asking 'Will I ever catch it in you some other time,'" he said calmly, and with that, he and Ralph were off to school.

Chapter Seven

Mr. Panikkos looked forward to explaining himself the following Friday evening. On previous occasions he had noticed that, whenever he had attempted to convey his ideas to Jill, she either found difficulty understanding him or openly contested what he said. And so now he was determined to speak as simply and as clearly as he could, because this particular idea seemed especially important to him.

Jill, Fran and Laura seemed rather fatigued, and not particularly eager for a discussion of the topic Mr. Panikkos had in mind.

"Do you remember the conversation we had last Friday night?" Mr. Panikkos asked. "Could we go back to it again for a moment?" He thought he saw Jill nudge Laura a bit with her foot, but he couldn't be sure, so he continued, "You made the statement, Laura, that men have minds and animals don't, isn't that right?"

Laura would have liked to say, "Just forget it, Mr. Panikkos," but instead she merely murmured, "Yes, I guess so."

Mr. Panikkos thought he now had their attention, so he went on, more briskly: "Well now, Laura, there is no sharp difference in intelligence between men and animals, in my opinion. It's just a difference of degree, much as the intellectual difference between human infants and human adults is only a difference of degree."

"I'm not sure I understand what you mean by 'a difference of degree,' " said Fran.

Jill and Laura nodded, indicating that they too wanted an explanation. Mr. Panikkos was surprised. He had taken it for granted that everyone was familiar with the distinction between "differences of degree' and "differences of kind." After a moment of reflection, he observed, "You are all of different heights, aren't you? Fran is tallest, and Laura is next tallest, and then comes Jill. So you differ when it comes to height, and these are differences of degree."

"Oh, we know that, Dad!" Jill exclaimed. "We're not altogether stupid, you know! And of course it's the same thing with weight. We were just talking about our weight when you came in. Fran weighs slightly more than I do, and Laura weighs slightly more than Fran. So that's another example of difference of degree."

"Excellent, excellent," said Mr. Panikkos, rubbing his hands in satisfaction. "And of course, the difference between height and weight is itself a difference of kind. It's not a gradual difference. It's a sharp difference. You measure height in inches and feet, while weight is measured in ounces and pounds. So they're really not comparable."

"What's that got to do with minds?" Fran asked, rather bluntly.

"Well, as I said before," Mr. Panikkos explained, "the difference between the mental behavior of the animal and that of man is, in my opinion, only a difference of degree, so we really can't say that animals lack minds, can we now?"

"But isn't the difference of degree between humans and animals so great as to be a difference of kind?" Jill asked, sipping her diet soda while holding a potato chip poised in the air.

"To be sure," replied Mr. Panikkos, pressing the tips of his fingers together. "Man has a culture, but do animals have a culture?" Before anyone could respond, he continued, "I know what you're going to ask: 'What's a culture?' Well, it's all the different ways of living together that a people in a particular society have developed. It's their language, and their educational system, and their religion, and their arts, the ways in which they make a living, the ways they organize their political systems, their marriages, their properties, and so on. And these different ways of living together are then handed down from one generation to the next. In this way, a culture comes to represent all the different life-experiences of hundreds of thousands of generations."

Fran, Jill and Laura sat looking at Mr. Panikkos. He realized that an illustration was in order, and suddenly he thought of one. "Jill," he said, "human beings travel naturally by land. What do they do when they wish to travel by water?"

"They swim—or they build ships," Jill answered, rather listlessly.

"And once someone has figured out how to build a ship, isn't it true that anyone else wishing to travel by water can copy his invention?" Mr. Panikkos asked, looking directly at Laura. "What's more, if people wish to fly, must they wait until they develop wings?"

"No," Laura laughed, "they invent airplanes or rockets. Or they use someone else's invention."

"But think about how different other creatures are," Mr. Panikkos remarked. "Birds fly, but they don't invent airplanes. Fish travel by water, but they don't build boats. As a matter of fact, whales once were land creatures, as you know, but they gradually *became* sea creatures. They survived not, like Noah, by *making* boats, but, one might say, by *becoming* boats—"

"Wait a minute," Fran broke in. "I think I'm beginning to see what you're driving at. Animals just *do* certain kinds of things. They live and travel in certain set ways. But man can invent new ways of living and new ways of changing the world around him."

"Uh-huh, you do understand!" Mr. Panikkos sat back in his chair and smiled.

Jill exclaimed, "Maybe she does, but I don't! What do boats and airplanes have to do with culture?"

Jill's father-in-law observed her patiently. "Don't you see, Jill," he said, "animals don't invent things. Yet people do, and all the inventions that all the people who've ever lived have made—all of them remain fixed for all time in human culture. Every time we use an invention or read a book or study a science or listen to music, we're enjoying someone else's idea—someone who may have lived thousands of years ago, and thousands of miles from here. Just as your memories are fixed in your mind, so the thoughts of mankind are established in human culture and will never disappear or die out."

Jill would have liked to protest that, in her opinion, animals *do* sometimes invent things. And Fran was prepared to assert that most of the original ideas people have invented have been lost rather than saved. But Laura got up to leave, and that terminated the evening's conversation.

* * *

By Monday, Jill could no longer recall the details of her father-in-law's theory of the mind. She tried telling Lisa and Harry about it, yet all she seemed able to relate to them was the distinction between differences of degree and differences of kind. To her surprise, it interested Harry and Lisa very much.

- "Lisa," Harry said, "remember how we turned those sentences around, and found that we *could* turn sentences around that began with the word 'no,' but we *couldn't* turn them around if they began with 'all'?
- Well, look. Here's what Jill's father said:

    Fran is taller than Laura.

    Laura is taller than Jill.

  Can we turn these sentences around? Of course not. Because if it's true that Fran is taller than Laura, then it
- just *can't* be true that Laura is taller than Fran."

  "Okay, I see what you mean," said Lisa. "But suppose you take a sentence like:

    New York is far from San Francisco.

  If you turn it around, it will still be true."
- "So these sentences are just like 'all' and 'no' sentences," Harry exclaimed, "only they don't begin with 'all' and 'no'!"

  Lisa looked perplexed. Then she said slowly, "Harry, could it be that what we're talking about this time are
- *relationships?*"

"What relationships?" Harry said, looking equally puzzled.

"I mean, like in arithmetic, where we use 'equals' and 'is greater than' and 'is smaller than.' Those are relationships, okay? And we know you can turn a sentence containing 'equals' around and it will still be true, but if you turn the others around, they'll become false."

"So in these kinds of sentences, it's relationships that count! Some relationships stay true when reversed, some become false!" Harry exclaimed, obviously delighted with their accomplishment.

At this point Jill, who had said nothing during the entire conversation, put in, "And what about a sentence like, 'Ben Beck is mad at Harry'? Can it be turned around?"

Before Harry could answer, he caught sight of someone standing in the doorway. It was Ben Beck, looking very disturbed. An instant later, he was gone.

Chapter Eight

The class could not begin on time because Kevin was trying to fix a slide projector he had been planning to use that evening. The members of the group were seated at their desks waiting for the session to begin. What were they thinking of while they waited?

Melissa Weinstein wondered if she was as indifferent towards her own children as her parents had been towards her.

Tom Schultz was trying to make a resolution not to drink when he got home in the evening.

- *Darrel Thompson* was considering going home because of the pain in his stomach.

- *Tony Basilio* was trying to figure out if there was an orderly sequence to the street numbers of the express subway stops: 14, 34, 42, 72, 96 . . .

  Suki Chen was thinking fondly of her friend, Penny, whom she had grown up with, but who had moved away many, many years ago.

- *Rudy Garlock* was imagining himself stepping out of a rocket ship—the first person to set foot on Mars. (There would be great caves to explore, filled with crystals of unbelievably beautiful colors.)

- *Luther Winfield* was trying not to think of the huge rat which had run across his bed the night before and which he then saw on the water pipe when he turned on the light. He was sure the rat had sniffed his face for a moment.

- *Mike Morawski* was amusing himself with an image of an encounter with Laura O'Reilly as she was unlocking her car door. He would hold her and kiss her.

Ann Torbrandtson was thinking what a lovely painting could be made of the vase of flowers on the window ledge.

Jennifer Starr was thinking of the violent argument she had had with her husband that morning. She'd given him the tiniest push and he stupidly fell over the coffee table and hurt his arm.

Pam Roberts wondered if her son would ever come home.

Mark Wallenda debated with himself about what he could do to protect his daughter, Mary, from the loungers and drifters she had to pass on her way to and from school each day.

Maria Atley considered the possibility that even after she finished the TALE course, she might not be able to find a better job.

Fran Woodson tried to decide what her main reason was for liking Kevin: that he was a nice person, that he was a good teacher, or that he was also Black.

Sam da Silva re-examined his options and concluded

- there was no way he could afford a VHS, even though there were some home movies he was dying to see.

- *Jill Panikkos* was marvelling at how perfect the whole world was. "How wonderful," she thought, "that the sky should be blue. Blue is just perfect! Of course, if it were green or purple or orange, they're nice colors, too, and they'd be equally perfect. I can't help feeling that whatever is, is right!" Then she added, "But a totally different world could be just as wonderful."

- And *Laura O'Reilly* was wondering how she might persuade her daughter to do her homework instead of talking endlessly on the telephone about boys.

- A few minutes later, as Harry and Lisa continued chatting together, what were the other members of the class thinking about?

Melissa Weinstein was wondering if she loved her children too much or too little.

Tom Schultz resolved not to drink that evening, but if he did, not to drink much.

- *Darrel Thompson* pondered the question whether an

emotional disturbance he was experiencing had caused his stomach to be upset, or the other way around.

Tony Basilio tried to figure out what Lisa could possibly say that Harry might find so interesting.

Suki Chen wondered if she should cut her hair, which fell, straight and black, down to her waist. But her father had liked it like that.

Rudy Garlock continued his exploration of a cave that led to the center of Mars. (It opened into an enormous room, lit by mysterious lights.)

Luther Winfield was still trying not to think of the rat. He shuddered.

Mike Morawski decided it wouldn't be right just to walk up to Laura and kiss her. He would say hello to her first.

"The shape of the stems and flowers in the vase is beautiful," *Anne Torbrandtson* thought, "but the colors are awful. If I were to paint it, I'd put in my own colors, and they'd be much better."

Jennifer Starr came to the conclusion that she had the

worst marriage in the world.

Pam Roberts recalled how happy her son was, even as an infant, and how he would squeal with laughter when she'd throw him up in the air and catch him. She wondered now if she might never see him again.

Mark Wallenda speculated how nice the world would be if there were no more wars and everyone had enough to eat.

Maria Atley's thoughts drifted back to her dissatisfaction with her present job. She couldn't decide if the fault lay with it or with her.

Fran Woodson remembered how she had said, "Why not?" when her daughter had asked her if a woman could ever become president of the United States. And the way she hesitated and then replied, "Why not?" again when her daughter asked, "Even a Black woman?"

Sam da Silva puzzled over why some people seemed to have lots of money and yet he had so little. He decided to save up enough for a lottery ticket, and then when he won, he'd buy a Ferrari racing car.

Jill Panikkos planned a trip to the shopping mall.

And *Laura O'Reilly* wondered if she was just imagining that Tony Basilio kept looking in her direction.

Kevin finally gave up on the slide projector, and the evening session was about to begin. Harry put the thought of Ben Beck's strange appearance out of his mind. He asked Kevin if they could spend a few moments on the three types of sentences. When Kevin raised his eyebrows a bit, Harry backtracked and asked, "Well, couldn't we just put the names of the first two kinds of sentences on the board and then make up lists of examples?"

After hesitating briefly, Kevin said, "Okay, first column—some examples of relationships that can be reversed."

"Equals," Lisa proposed. "For instance, 'Three plus seven *equals* ten.' Turn it around and it's still true: 'Ten *equals* three plus seven.' "

"I know! I know!" shouted Mike. "Greater than! Six

- is *greater than* two, and when you . . . turn . . . it. . ."

Everyone laughed, even Kevin.

"How about 'is a sister of'?" asked Suki. "If it's true that, say, 'Joan *is a sister of* Mary,' then it's true that
- 'Mary *is a sister of* Joan.' "

"Sounds okay," was Lisa's opinion.

But Kevin paused and Harry quickly said, "No, no, wait! Take my kids: Linda *is the sister of* Tyrone, but Tyrone isn't *the sister of* Linda."
- Now Mike had his hand up again. "This time I've got it," he announced. "*Un*equal to! If it's true that nine *is unequal to* five, then it's also true that five *is unequal to* nine."

A scattering of applause was Mike's reward, and in
- appreciation, he stood up and bowed handsomely until Sam, who was sitting next to him, pulled him down.

Laura then suggested "a long way from." "Because," she said, "if my house is *a long way from* where Lisa lives, then where Lisa lives is *a long way*
- *from* my house."

Kevin thought it would be all right now to go on to the next column: relationships that can't be turned around. "Let's put down Mike's first suggestion, 'greater than,' as our first example. Any others?"

Suki had been thinking of her own previous proposal. "You know," she said, "if I had suggested 'is a cousin of,' I would have been right. But that's okay. I can think of something: sentences with 'is the father of.' If Mr. Panikkos *is the father of* Joe, then it would be false to say that Joe *is the father of* Mr. Panikkos."

"Is stronger than," said Darrel. Kevin nodded agreement, and wrote, "is stronger than" in the second column.

The attention of some members of the class had begun to waver, and several conversations were starting up. Harry called over to Darrel and Mike, "Hey, you guys, cool it for a minute!"

Mike just grinned and replied, "Cool it yourself, Prime Time!"

But Harry was thinking about the sentences that had

- been written on the board earlier:

    Fran is taller than Laura.

    Laura is taller than Jill.

  "Look," said Harry, "if you put these two sentences
- together, you can see that Fran is taller than Jill."

  "Aw, everybody knows that," said Mike. "All you have to do is look and you can see that Fran's a head taller than Jill."

  "What I mean," replied Harry, "is that you don't
- have to put their *heads* together. You can just put the two *sentences* together and you can see it."

  Tony shrugged. "It's obvious!" he asserted. "If 8 is bigger than 6, and 6 is bigger than 4, then obviously 8 is bigger than 4. What's so wonderful about that?"

- Lisa said quietly, "I think Harry's point is that some relationships like 'is bigger than,' sort of *carry over,* while others don't."

  "It seems to me that 'gets up earlier than' is the kind that carries over," said Maria. "Because if I *get up*
- *earlier than* Melissa, and Melissa *gets up earlier than*

Anne, then it must be true that I *get up earlier than* Anne."

Sam suggested "richer than," and Tom suggested, "busier than." While Kevin was writing them down on the board, Mike suggested "smarter than," but Kevin said "I think we have enough now, Mike," before Mike could illustrate his suggestion.

"Now, how about examples of the kind that don't carry over?" Kevin asked.

"Daughter of," said Fran. "If Mindy's *the daughter of* Patricia and Patricia's *the daughter of* Louise, it still isn't the case that Mindy's *the daughter of* Louise."

"How about 'five years older than'?" Jennifer put in. "Because if I'm *five years older than* my sister Edna, and Edna's *five years older than* my brother Peter, it still doesn't follow that I'm only *five years older than* Peter."

Kevin thought it was time he got on with the regular lesson. But Harry found it difficult to pay attention. He kept thinking about the carry-over type of relationships.

- Then he knew what it was: the sentences in his notebook—"All history lessons are interesting," and so on. But did the word "are" stand for a carry-over relationship? He decided to try it. Suppose we take the sentence,
- "All history lessons are classes," he reflected, and we add to it, "All classes are interesting," what do we get? Obviously, Harry decided, we get, "All history lessons are interesting."

Harry felt he had caught on to something important.
- He decided to try it again. He took two sentences:

>All spaniels are dogs.

>All dogs are animals.

What must follow, Harry thought, is "All spaniels are animals," because the relationship was one that carried
- over. The word "are," Harry figured, must mean something like "belong to the class of," or "are members of the class of." "I guess saying, 'All spaniels are dogs' is pretty much the same thing as saying, 'All spaniels belong to the class of dogs.' So sentences with the word
- 'are' are carry-over sentences," he concluded.

A week went by before Harry had any reason to think about carry-over relationships again. He was doing a cross-word puzzle, and 39 down was "British islands." There were eight blank spaces, and Harry happened to think of the word "Shetland." He knew the Shetland Islands were where Shetland ponies came from, but he had no idea where the Shetland Islands were on the map.

Harry consulted an encyclopedia. It said only that the Shetland Islands were a part of Scotland. But that was all Harry needed to know. It was a fact that Scotland was a part of Great Britain, so it had to be that the Shetland Islands were also a part of Great Britain. He wrote it down:

The Shetland Islands are a part of Scotland.
Scotland is a part of Great Britain.
_____

Therefore, the Shetland Islands are a part
of Great Britain.

Somewhere in Harry's mind, there was a vague doubt about what he had done. He halfway perceived that "are a part of" might not work the same way as "are." It might not be a carry-over relationship. But Harry's thoughts were tumbling about, one after the other, and he couldn't stop them long enough to examine the "are a part of" relationship. "We can take two carry-over sentences and from them we can figure out a third sentence," he mused. "And yet—do people really think this way?" He remembered Tony's comment: "So what?—what good is all this?" And for the first time Harry felt a little annoyed. What good was mathematics or geometry or grammar or history? What good was anything? If thinking about how to add and subtract correctly or how to speak correctly was good, thinking about how to think correctly was good, too! It was a little while before he cooled down.

* * *

Tony and Mark stopped off in Toohey's Bar for a beer after class. After talking about football for a while, Tony asked, "Did you tell Harry what really happened the day he almost got sideswiped by a car?"

Mark shook his head. "All I told him was that it might have been Ben Beck. Why? What really happened?"

Tony sipped his beer slowly, then said, "Well, y'know, Ben was in Viet Nam, and I guess he went through some of the worst of it there. I don't know—it's hard to tell why some things set some people off. But first he overheard Harry talking about his kids, and that seemed to bother him. Then, all through the next class, Harry kept talking about what sentences follow from what sentences—you know the way he talks. And it seemed to bug Ben more and more. So anyhow, I was walking out the side door that night, and when I'd gotten almost to the sidewalk, I heard Ben behind me, muttering to himself about Harry. The next thing I knew, he was driving down the street, and Harry was standing by the curb, and Ben's car almost touched Harry as it went past."

"Why didn't you tell Harry?" Mark asked. "For a

- while there, he thought *you* were the driver."

"I was waiting for him to accuse me," Tony replied, "but he never did."

Mark finished off his beer and said, "I think you'd
- better tell him what you just told me. I think he should know."

Chapter Nine

The evening session had not yet begun, and Darrel Thompson was deep in conversation with Kevin in a corner of the room. As Darrel spoke, his voice shook, and it was evident that he was very troubled. Kevin listened silently but sympathetically. Finally he remarked, "Darrel, I have no idea what to say to you. But I'll tell you what: if you'd like to present your problem to the class, go ahead. Maybe they can help you."

The members of the class were silent as Darrel, sitting on the desk at the front of the room where Kevin usually sat, struggled to compose himself enough to begin. This was the story he told:

"Some of you may know that I have a son, Dale, who's twelve years old, and who's been attending P.S. 14. For the past month, Dale's regular teacher has been out sick, and they've had a substitute, a Mrs. Cudahy, in her place.

"Every morning the kids are expected to salute the flag, or at least to stand during the salute. But the other day, when it was time for the salute of the flag, Dale didn't stand up. When the teacher asked him why, he couldn't give a reason.

"After a while, Mrs. Cudahy sent Dale downstairs to see the principal, Mr. Partridge. Dale had to sit in the outer office for almost a half hour until Mr. Partridge was free to see him. It was a very miserable half hour.

"Mr. Partridge said, 'Well, now, Dale, what seems to be the trouble?' His voice was friendly and Dale, who had been sitting there crying, began drying his face with his handkerchief and blowing his nose.

"Between sniffles, Dale blurted out, 'I couldn't, Mr. Partridge, I just couldn't. My parents told me I mustn't.'

"Mr. Partridge looked at Dale very seriously. He said, 'Your parents? Why should they object to your standing during the salute?'

"Dale answered, 'It's their religion—it's our religion. My father showed it to me last night in the Bible. It's in Chapter 20 of Exodus. It forbids idolatry.' What Dale told Mr. Partridge was correct: it was just what happened. I showed him the passage in the Bible.

"Anyhow, Mr. Partridge asked Dale what he thought 'idolatry' meant. Dale said, 'That's what I asked my father, and he told me it was 'bowing down to images.' He showed me where it said, 'Thou shalt have no other gods before me.' He said that it would be like bowing down to a false god.'

"So then, Dale told me, Mr. Partridge spoke to him very gently. 'Dale,' he said, 'the United States flag isn't an image of anything. It's just an—an emblem or symbol. And standing up is not the same thing as bowing down to a god or to the image of a god. It's just a gesture of respect for what the flag stands for.'

" 'What's it stand for?' Dale asked.

"Mr. Partridge told him, 'Why, the country—Dale, you know that perfectly well.'

"At this, Dale couldn't face Mr. Partridge, so he just stared at the floor. 'Well, maybe we aren't worshipping the flag itself,' he said. 'Maybe what we do is worship the country the flag represents, and that's what my father and mother object to, because they say we're supposed to worship God and nothing else.'

"I guess this stopped Mr. Partridge for a moment, but finally he said, 'I'll tell you what, Dale. You go back to your room, and as soon as I get a chance, I'd like to come down to talk to your class about this, since they all saw it happen this morning, and they might be upset about it.'

"I guess that's pretty much what happened, and it's pretty much what I told Kevin a few minutes ago. I don't know what to do about it, and he thought I could maybe throw it out for a discussion this evening and maybe get some ideas from you about what I can do."

Laura asked, "Do you think Mr. Partridge is going to discuss the matter with Dale's class?"

"Yes," Darrel responded, "that's exactly what he said he's going to do."

"I wish we could be there," said Lisa.

Fran added, "Or, I wish we could have Mr. Partridge here."

There was a momentary silence, then Harry spoke up. "Why couldn't we? Not for real, of course, but why couldn't we discuss the matter together *as if* he were here?"

"Without him here, it would never work!" Fran objected.

Harry appealed to Kevin: "Couldn't *you* play Mr. Partridge?"

Harry's plea amused Kevin and he replied, "Well, I guess it wouldn't hurt. I'll try." He went to the closet, found a tie and jacket, and in an instant had transformed himself into what he thought a principal might look like.

Clearing his throat loudly, Kevin began, "Now, class, as you know, Kevin's parents don't want him to stand during the salute of the flag. They have religious reasons. In my opinion, however, saluting the flag has nothing to do with religion."

Mark Wallenda raised his hand. "Mr. Partridge, you say it has nothing to do with religion. But when we pledge allegiance to the flag, we're supposed to mention God, and that seems to me to have something to do with religion."

"I didn't make up the words of the pledge," Kevin responded. "The wording of the pledge is standard, and children recite them the same way in all the schools of the state."

Mark was unable to reply, and just sat shaking his head. But Maria spoke up firmly. "Dale," she said, looking straight at Darrel, "I definitely think your parents are wrong. Because it's just like Mr. Partridge here says: everybody does this, stands during the salute. And no one else sees anything wrong with it, so why shouldn't you do the same thing?"

"The fact that everyone—or almost everyone—does something doesn't make it right," Darrel answered.

Maria insisted, "But this is the law of the country!"

"My parents tell me that Divine laws come first," Darrel responded softly.

"I don't know," said Ben Beck, from the back of the room. Everyone turned towards him as he continued, "Can parents ever be wrong?"

Darrel said, "The Bible tells us we're to honor our parents. Would I be honoring them if I disagreed with them about what the Bible tells me to do?"

"But Dale," said Kevin, "couldn't this all be just a matter of how we are to *interpret* the Bible? Your parents are entitled to their own interpretation, of course, but they could be wrong, couldn't they?"

"Sure, they could," replied Darrel. "But just because they're in a minority doesn't mean they *have* to be

- wrong. Those who are the majority could also be wrong, just as easily."

   Kevin decided to try another approach. "As you probably know, Dale," he said, "there are people who are
- sure they know what the Bible means—maybe your parents are among these—and they believe that the Bible forbids blood transfusions. Now suppose you were very sick, and were going to die unless you could get a blood transfusion. Would it still be right for your
- parents to object?"

   Darrel hung his head and said merely, "I don't know, Mr. Partridge."

   "So you'll ask your parents to come see me about this?" Kevin urged.
- All Darrel would say was, "I'll talk to them tonight about it."

   But Tony Basilio wasn't inclined to let the matter drop just yet. "Dale," he said, "a moment ago you said you wouldn't be honoring your parents if you disagreed
- with them. Did the Bible tell you that, or is it something

you figured out for yourself?"

"I guess I figured it out for myself," Darrel answered.

"And as you yourself have already admitted," Tony continued, "you could be wrong, couldn't you?"

"Sure, I could," said Darrel, "but how?"

"Well, isn't it possible," Tony asked, "that it's no dishonor to disagree with someone?"

"I don't get you," Darrel protested.

"Take Kevin," said Tony, at which Kevin flushed a bit. "He actually *likes* us to disagree with him. He *wants* us to have questions about what he teaches us, and even if we come to conclusions that are different from his, he still seems to respect us."

"That's right," put in Rudy Garlock. "Remember that time he told us that we ought to compete with ideas in the classroom the way athletes compete in sports? I think Kevin actually feels honored if we disagree with him!"

Kevin looked up at the ceiling with a saintly expression for a moment, then resumed his role as Mr. Partridge. "I believe you have something there, boys," he said. "Dale, I'd never counsel you to do something that went against your religious principles. Nor would I tell you that you ought to disagree with your parents. But when you talk with them tonight, couldn't you try to make them see that you wouldn't be dishonoring them if you came to your own conclusions?"

Darrel was silent, but now Mike Morawski was waving his arm frantically, and Kevin nodded to him. "Mr. Partridge, " Mike said, "it works both ways."

"What works both ways?" asked Kevin.

"I mean," said Mike, "if Dale's parents are to feel honored at his disagreeing with them, then you should feel honored at our disagreeing with you. And in fact, even if we do something that's the opposite of what everyone else is doing, if what we think we're doing is right, and if we can say why we think it's right, then we really aren't disrespectful in doing it."

"But suppose what you're doing is something that

hurts other people, what then?" Maria wanted to know.

"I didn't say we should hurt other people," Mike protested. "But if it's a matter of standing up during some ceremonies, and if I really thought it was wrong for me to do it, and if just the same everyone else wanted me to do it and forced me to do it, then they'd be hurting me a lot more than I'd be hurting them."

"Mike," said Kevin, shaking his head, "there are some things that people expect of you, and we in the schools wouldn't be doing our duty if we didn't try to show you what's expected of you. We try to make good citizens of you because society expects you to be good citizens when you finish school. I know it isn't easy to accept that fact, just as it isn't easy to swallow some bad-tasting medicine. But just as you'll be a healthier person for swallowing the medicine, so you'll be a better person for accepting what I've told you."

Harry Prime couldn't resist making a comment of his own. "Mike and Tony weren't asking you to do what was better just for *them,* Mr. Partridge. They were asking you to do what would be better for *everyone.*"

"You mean freedom to do as you please?" asked Kevin gravely.

"I guess what I mean," said Harry, "is that kids need to be free to think for themselves just as much as grown-ups do, maybe more so."

"Well," said Kevin, "take this matter of Dale's not standing. I could have tried to settle it privately, but instead I brought it to all of you here for a free and open discussion. Is that the sort of thing you want?"

"It's a start," said Harry.

No one had anything to add. Finally Lisa remarked, "It was good of you to provide Mr. Partridge's point of view, Kevin, whatever you may have thought of it privately." Kevin nodded, but said nothing.

Then Darrel remarked, simply, "I thought it went very well. Now my wife and I have got to decide what to do."

Chapter Ten

If Kevin thought that the discussion of the problem posed by Darrel Thompson was finished, he was mistaken. The following week, the classroom buzzed with conversation, as if the members of the class had hardly been able to wait to express the opinions they had developed. Tony had his hand up. "What is it, Tony?" Kevin asked, frowning a bit.

"Look," Tony said, in that clear and distinct way he had of talking, "a lot of us have things we'd like to say about Dale Thompson's situation. Could we continue the discussion we had last week?"

"I'm sorry, Tony," Kevin responded. "I know that many of you have had this on your minds, but we have a grammar lesson to finish and we still haven't discussed your writing assignments. I think we'd better get on with the regular schedule."

Harry Prime spoke up. "But Tony has a point, Kevin. Would it really be different from what we're trying to do in this course? Look, you acted Mr. Partridge last week. Couldn't you act like a referee or something this evening, and you can criticize the way we express ourselves."

"That's very ingenious, Harry," said Kevin, "but I can criticize your ways of expressing yourselves when I go over your assignments."

"Well, then," said Harry, still not giving up, "how about criticizing the way we reason? We'll give our opinions, and you can tell us whether we're thinking well or thinking badly."

Kevin sighed. "Just tonight—and after that, no more?"

"Just tonight," Tony and Harry assured him together.

"Very well, then," said Kevin, folding up his notebook. "Who wants to speak first?"

Surprisingly, Melissa Weinstein was the first to speak up. "I think Darrel's son should stand up during the salute like everyone else," she said.

"Why?" asked Kevin.

"Why?" repeated Melissa.

"Yes, why, Melissa? You can't just state your opinion. You have to give a reason for it. Anyone can have an opinion, but I can't tell if you're reasoning well or badly unless you tell me why you think the way you do."

Melissa looked up anxiously at Kevin and said, "But I don't think I have a reason. I just know how I feel."

"Well," said Kevin, "when you've figured out your reason for feeling the way you do, let us know. Who's next?"

"I'll tell you why he should stand up," Ben Beck announced. "The whole country's in terrible shape. All sorts of bad things are happening. It's like a powder keg: one little spark and the whole place is liable to blow up. So I don't think we can allow people just to go around doing as they please."

Kevin didn't respond immediately. He obviously had to give Ben Beck's remarks much consideration. Finally he replied, "Ben, at first I thought what you said was a pretty good argument for your opinion. But the more I think it over, the more I'm convinced it isn't. Because really, Ben, you're not trying to *persuade* us to agree with you. You're trying to *frighten* us into agreeing with you. First you tell us you're alarmed at the world situation, and then you say that *therefore* Dale ought to be made to stand up. But it doesn't follow, because you haven't shown how these things are connected. And, you haven't shown that everything is more likely to explode if Dale *doesn't* stand up during the salute."

The members of the class weren't discouraged by Kevin's criticisms of the first two expressions of opinion. They were used to his being severe with them when it came to reading and writing well.

The next person to speak was Jill Panikkos: "I think Dale ought to stick by his beliefs because—because that's what my husband says, and he ought to know."

"What do you mean, 'he ought to know,' Jill? Is he a lawyer or a judge or an authority of some kind?" Kevin asked.

"No, but he's awful smart," Jill said, with obvious admiration.

"Well," said Kevin, "I'm sorry, but that won't do. It just won't do. You should only use someone else's opinion as a reason for your own view if that other person is a recognized authority on the subject in question."

Jill wasn't happy with Kevin's judgment, but she said nothing.

Suki Chen volunteered that Dale should be made to stand up, because "rules are rules."

Again Kevin had to pause and reflect before responding. Then he said, "Suki, I'm going to accept that, even though technically it's wrong. What I mean is that a statement like 'rules are rules' ordinarily doesn't mean very much. It's like saying 'wallpaper is wallpaper' or 'stones are stones.' But sometimes it's used as a familiar expression or idiom with a definite meaning that everyone understands, like 'business is business.' In this case, I suppose what you mean is that if we make rules, we should keep them. So I'll have to say okay."

Now Mike's hand was up. "No," he insisted, "rules are made to be broken. Don't you know the expression, 'every rule has an exception'? Well, Dale's case is the exception! That's why I think Dale doesn't have to stand if he doesn't want to."

Kevin looked somewhat pained, but he said, "All right, Mike, I suppose that if I allowed Suki to use an idiomatic expression, I'll have to allow you to do the same. But I still think that what you've told me is a pretty poor excuse for a reason."

Mike looked so hurt that Laura started to laugh, then clapped her hand over her mouth. But Tony wanted to be heard. "Kevin, maybe Mike didn't say it so well, but I don't think what he said was as bad as you made it out to be."

"How do you mean, Tony?" asked Kevin.

"Well, lots of times we'll say that something or other is *always* true, and yet we know it really isn't. I mean, we know there are exceptions, but we still talk as if there weren't any. For example, I'll say something like, 'all wood floats.' And yet I know that ebony doesn't float, and it's a wood."

Kevin nodded his approval of Tony's remark, then looked around the room. "Okay, who wants to be next?"

Sam da Silva seldom spoke up in class, but now he seemed to have an idea he just *had* to express. "I think," he said in his drawling fashion, "we keep forgetting one thing. Kids don't *choose* to go to school. They're *made* to go to school. And we don't choose our religions. They're given to us when we're born—"

"For that matter," interrupted Ben Beck, "we don't choose our parents."

"And for *that* matter," added Jennifer Starr, "we don't even choose to be born! I know *I* didn't!"

Kevin tapped with his pencil on the desk. "Please. Let Sam finish what he was saying."

"It's okay, Kevin," said Sam. "They were only trying to help me out. What I'm trying to say is that sometimes we don't mind being told what to do, and sometimes we *do* mind, you know what I mean? I mean like, when I was a kid, I always wanted to join the Blue Falcons. The Blue Falcons! Wow, you do what they tell you! They tell you to jump from the roof of one building to another, you jump! They tell you to push one of the Wharf Rats around, you push him around! But the thing is, I joined the Blue Falcons because I wanted to. I didn't especially like doing those things, but if you choose to belong, you do them."

"That's very interesting, Sam, but what's the point you're trying to make?" Kevin inquired.

Sam shrugged. "I don't know. I mean, I know, but I can't say what I mean any better than I just said it."

Tony spoke up: "I think I can tell you what he means. He means that if you belong to a group, like a gang, of your own free will, then you really have to do anything they tell you. But if you're a member of a group that you didn't choose to belong to, then they shouldn't make you do things you really don't want to do."

"But be specific," Kevin urged. "How does this relate to Dale?"

"It means that since Dale didn't choose to belong to his religion, he shouldn't have to do things it tells him to do if he thinks it's wrong to do them," Tony said.

"Yes," said Mark, "but it also means that since he doesn't go to school of his own free will, he shouldn't have to do what the school tells him to do, either, if he really thinks it wrong."

Jennifer Starr looked questioningly at Tony and Mark. "And does that go for our families, too? After all, as Ben said just a moment ago, we don't choose our families."

"I think what it comes down to is a matter of trust,"

- said Fran. "I agree with what they're saying, mostly. But you generally trust your own family. You didn't choose them, but they chose you, and you know they love you. With strangers, it's different."

- "Lots of times when I'm with strangers, I trust them," Jane remarked. "But families can be awful mean sometimes."

  "Sure," Fran replied, "but then they're like Sam's Blue Falcons—you do what they want because you want
- to continue to belong with them."

  Kevin thought over what had been said, and then commented, "I've never thought of it quite like that before. Thank you very much, all of you."

  And Darrel, who had been listening quietly all even-
- ing, without saying so much as a single word, echoed Kevin softly: "Thank you very much, all of you."

Chapter Eleven

The class should already have begun, but Kevin was late. The members of the group at the TALE center, usually talkative, sat about silently, these thoughts uppermost in their minds:

Melissa Weinstein: "Imagine Kevin saying *he* learned something from *us*! I never heard a teacher say that sort of thing before. Or a parent either. I'll never forget how, when I'd ask my father or mother anything, they'd have an answer ready before I'd even finished my question. It's funny—the moment Kevin said that, I felt like

- more of a person, like I knew who I was a little better."

  Tom Schultz: "I can feel for Darrel's kid. I can just imagine what it must be like sitting in class and having everyone talk about *my* problem."

- *Tony Basilio:* "The other day I said to my kid, 'I wish everything in the world were as simple and clear and distinct and true as arithmetic is. When things are exact and precise, there are no contradictions, so there are no arguments. But in the real world, there's always some-

- one saying the opposite of someone else.' So he said, 'Aw, Dad, a fact's a fact,' and I said, 'I can't think of a single fact I know to be absolutely true.' He didn't say anything. He just got out his arithmetic book, so I could help him with his homework. And when it asked for the

- square root of 2, he gave me this funny kind of look."

  Ben Beck: "I just can't believe my ears when I hear kids nowadays talk about their 'rights.' They really don't have rights; they just have duties. And what's so wrong about that? I don't mind standing up to salute the flag!

- I love the flag! I enjoy saluting it and I get goose

pimples every time someone sings the *Star Spangled Banner* just before a ball game. People *should* love their country, just like they should love their home and their parents. In fact, we call it our 'mother country,' don't we? So it's really like another parent to us. I remember my mother as perfect: I'll never have a disrespectful thought about her. So I can't understand how anyone would want to show disrespect for his country by refusing to stand up during the salute to the flag."

Suki Chen: "That Anne Torbrandtson is really nice! She showed me a watercolor she did of the bowl of flowers in the window, and so I showed her a poem I'd written about snow on the windowsills. After she'd read it, I read it over and over again to myself. Somehow, when a person you like reads what you've written and says they like it, it seems all fresh and new afterwards. I wonder why."

Rudy Garlock: "They say Ben Beck was going with someone last year, and they were supposed to get married, and she got killed in an auto accident. I wonder how it feels to have that sort of thing happen to you."

Luther Winfield: "Mike and I went bowling the other night, and he said to me afterwards, 'Hey, Luther, tell me, what's it feel like to be black?' and I said to him, 'Man, what's it feel like to be white?' Then he laughed and said, 'I guess it really doesn't make much difference one way or the other, does it?' But it does. If I were short and fat, like Mike, I'd be a different person. I can't even imagine myself short and fat. I guess I'm black in the same way I'm tall and skinny. Or maybe I'm Black the same way I'm American."

Mike Morawski: "Laura O'Reilly strikes me as the kind of girl who only goes out with wimps, because they're safe. But I'll bet she'd really appreciate a *real* man for a change, one who's all muscle, even if he happened to be a couple of inches shorter than her."

Anne Torbrandtson: "At first I couldn't figure Suki out. I couldn't read her face. Then I thought, 'Maybe she has a secret.' Now I know what it is. She feels things the way I do. When I read her poem, it was as if she had reached out her hand to me."

Jennifer Starr: "I've never been able to stay where I didn't feel wanted. That's why I ran away from home and that's why I've got to get away from Bud. I'm not going to stop with this high school certificate. I'm going right on to college. Who knows how far I'll go? But I've got to be on my own!"

Mark Wallenda: "Kevin's a great guy. I like him. I was put off at first because he seemed so laid back. But now I can tell he really thinks for himself. I'll bet he doesn't take all that religious stuff any more seriously than I do."

Maria Atley: "I'll never get over how strange it is to find myself in the same evening school class with Mark! We used to be together a lot when we were kids, because we lived next door to each other. But I've hardly ever seen him since then. It's funny: if you're unrelated, everything's clear-cut, and if you're brother and sister, everything's clear-cut. But being cousins is such a fuzzy relationship!"

- *Fran Woodson:* "I keep thinking about that poor kid of Darrel Thompson's. No one gives him a reason. All the principal can tell him is, 'That's the way it is because that's the way the Board of Education says it is.' And all
- Darrel can tell him is, 'That's the way it is because that's the way God says it is.' But shouldn't there be a reason for everything we're told to do? If we're told to do something and no reason is given, what reason do *we* have for doing it?"
- *Sam da Silva:* "When I talked the other day about the Blue Falcons, I didn't say anything about how scared I was. But whatever they told me, I believed. For example, they told me they were the only gang that was any good, so how could I doubt them? They were the great-
- est, so I figured whatever they said must be true. But it didn't keep me from being scared."

Jill Panikkos: "Everything my father-in-law says sets me off. Why do I let it bother me so much? I should have my own place and then this sort of thing wouldn't
- happen. But have I a right to break up the family?

Could we bear to get along without each other?''

Laura O'Reilly: ''All Jennifer thinks about is carving out a career for herself. That's why she takes these adult ed courses. But let's face it: all I'm here for is to find a guy I'll be happy with and to have a home and kids. And yet, why is it that even when I find them, I can't hold them? Is it because I don't want to be loved just for my green eyes and chestnut hair? Too bad Tony's married. I'll bet he could learn to appreciate me for my self alone, and not just for my looks.''

Pam Roberts: ''I wonder if I'm pregnant. That would certainly raise a lot of questions!''

Lisa Torrey: ''I'm such an ugly duckling that my mother and father were always afraid I'd throw myself at the first man who showed an interest in me. Well, that hasn't been so. I've been very choosy. But why is it that, even though Harry hasn't even once asked me out, I keep wondering what it would be like to be married to a guy who's been divorced and who has a couple of teen-age twins?''

- *Harry Prime:* "I've got to ask Lisa out. It would be a terribly big step, but I've just got to take it. I can't think any further ahead than that: one step at a time. It's really scary: what if she's already going with someone?
- What if she just laughs at me? And yet, how beautiful she is! And how often we seem to think about the same things, but differently! Still, even when we think differently, our ways of thinking are so—compatible!

  "And I'm really beginning to appreciate Kevin. He
- knows where it's at. He doesn't pretend to know what the truth is, but he doesn't hesitate a moment when it comes to telling someone he's guilty of sloppy reasoning. He probably knew all along we wouldn't come up with an idea that would save Darrel's kid, but he
- thought it worthwhile that we should at least try to talk about it.

  "I guess, in the long run, all I can do is try to tell the difference between thinking well and thinking badly, just like an umpire who stands behind the plate, and
- even though he can't pitch himself, he knows the dif-

ference between a ball and a strike."

Darrel Thompson: "In my opinion, kids who are in school have a constitutional right to be excused from doing something that their conscience or their parents tell them is wrong. If a regulation is immoral, then it would be immoral to obey it. I think we're just going to have to find another school for Dale."

Chapter Twelve

First Pam Roberts stopped coming to class. There was no word of explanation from her. Then Darrel Thompson announced that he had gotten a job in another community and would be moving away. He didn't say the move had anything to do with his son's problem in school, but many members of the class figured there was such a connection.

Harry usually got to class early, because he went there directly from work. Lisa didn't usually arrive until the session was about to begin, so he was surprised to see her saunter in early this particular evening.

"I feel badly about Darrel," she remarked, without any preliminary conversation. "We gave him no help."

"I know," Harry agreed. "I feel kind of ashamed about it. But it wasn't just a little problem which someone can't solve because he's stated it wrong. It was much too big for us to get a handle on and think about clearly."

Lisa shook her head. "You shouldn't feel as badly as the rest of us. At least you keep pushing us to think better about things like this."

The praise left Harry almost tongue-tied. She smiled at him, and he was enchanted by the remarkable way her large grey eyes contrasted with and yet balanced her pert nose and spaced-apart teeth. Fearful he might say something that would express how he felt, he turned desperately to his notebook and found the page on which, some weeks earlier, he had written down the four sample sentences that Kevin had put on the board:

All courses are interesting.

No courses are interesting.

Some courses are interesting.

Some courses are not interesting.

Harry scowled at the page. "We haven't accomplished anything in weeks," he said. "But where do we go from here?"

"Well," said Lisa, "we could go back to where we started: turning sentences around. Look, we found the first kind of sentence became false when reversed, but the second remained true. So what about the third and fourth kinds? It seems to me the third kind stays true, too. If some courses are interesting things, then some interesting things are courses. Here, let me show you on the board." Lisa proceeded to draw two intersecting circles, the first of which she labelled "courses," and the second she labelled "interesting things." She then numbered the three areas in the circles as 1, 2 and 3:

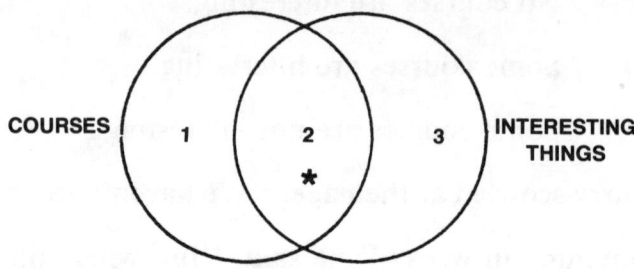

- "See," Lisa said, "the asterisk means that Area 2 is occupied. It means that some things in the *courses* circle are also in the *interesting things* circle. So you could read it either way, as 'Some courses are interesting things,' or as 'Some interesting things are courses.'"

- "Hey, that's neat!" Harry said, regarding Lisa with admiration. Let me try it with the fourth sentence:

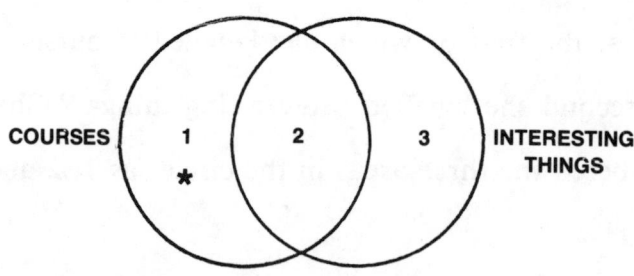

"Okay, look what happens," said Harry. "When you read the diagram from left to right, number one tells us that some courses are not interesting things. But when you read it from right to left, it doesn't tell us anything, because neither number 2 nor number 3 have asterisks. It certainly doesn't tell us that some interesting things are courses. In order for that to happen, there would have to be an asterisk in Area 2."

"But that's right!" Lisa exclaimed. "Suppose we took the sentence, 'Some animals are not lions.' If we turn it around, it becomes, 'Some lions are not animals.' The first one's true but the second's false."

"So what we've found out," said Harry, enthusiastically, "is that we can be sure the second and third kinds of sentences will stay true when reversed, but we can't be sure the first and fourth kinds will stay true when reversed!"

It came over them again that they had shared another discovery experience, and they each felt a bit awed at what had occurred. But it was left to Lisa to try to express how she felt about what was happening. "It's lovely, isn't it?" she asked softly.

Harry looked back at the circles on the board. It wouldn't have occurred to him to call them "lovely," he reflected. He turned his attention to the four sentences. "Y'know what, Lisa?" he observed. "They're opposites!" They're two pairs of opposites!" He wrote them out on the board:

All courses are interesting. ⬅———➡ Some courses are not interesting.

No courses are interesting. ⬅———➡ Some courses are interesting.

Lisa studied Harry for a moment and then, with a little smile, she remarked, "They're not just opposites, Harry, they're *contradictories*. If one of them is true, the other member of the pair has just *got* to be false!"

At that moment, for no particular reason, Lisa thought of Darrel, as he was when he said he wouldn't be coming back. Lisa had an image of each person in the class giving Darrel something by which they would be remembered. Then the image faded and she imagined Dale walking silently to the door, turning to wave for a

—134—

moment, and then disappearing into the night.

Somehow, everyone who was left in the class seemed more precious now than before, Lisa thought. They too, all of them, had shared an experience. It hadn't been pleasant, but it left her feeling distinctly more fond of the others than she had previously, and she wondered why.

* * *

"Luther, is that you?" Mrs. Winfield called from the kitchen.

"Yeah, Mom," Luther Winfield answered, "have you seen Jeremy?"

Mrs. Winfield called back, "No, haven't seen him since he went off to school this morning. He's usually back by this time. How about you—any luck today?"

Before Luther could answer, Jeremy came in. He was a mess. His shirt was torn at the shoulder, which was scratched and bleeding, and his clothes were all muddy.

"Hey, man," said Luther, "what happened to you?

You get in a fight or something?"

Jeremy was breathing hard, as if he'd been running. "No, that wasn't it. I got hit by a car."

"Come in here and let me look at that shoulder," said his grandmother.

"Aw, it's okay. It's all *right*! Nothing but a scratch," said Jeremy. "But my bike—" His voice shook and he couldn't continue.

"How'd it happen?" Luther asked.

"Well," said Jeremy, while his grandmother was helping him get his shirt off, "I was coming home on Main Avenue, and as I was getting to Highland Street, I saw this car coming pretty fast down Highland, but I figured he'd stop, because Highland is a stop street and I never had to worry about it. The cars coming down Highland *always* stop at the intersection with Main Avenue. So I just kept on peddling. And first thing I knew, that dude who was driving went right through the intersection, and his rear bumper caught my front wheel and practically ripped it off. I got thrown halfway across the street and almost hit a fire plug."

"Jeremy," Mrs. Winfield said, "I've *told* you to be careful . . ."

"I *was* careful, grandma, honest," said Jeremy, "but how did I know this crazy nut was going right through that stop sign?"

"Y'know," Luther remarked, "you just now said that *all* the cars coming down Highland stop at the Main Avenue intersection. But this one didn't. So what you said at first was wrong, wasn't it? You never know for sure what the other fellow's going to do."

Suddenly Luther remembered the discussion from the previous evening. What was it now? Someone had said that the contradiction of "All courses are interesting" is "Some courses are not interesting." And then someone else had said, "You only need one uninteresting course —just one, and that'll make the statement, 'All courses are interesting' false."

And now the same sort of thing had happened to Jeremy. He'd thought that all cars stop at the intersection.

- But this one didn't. One single exception and you can no longer say "all." "You gotta watch out for those crazy drivers," Luther said to Jeremy gently. "It only takes one."
- "That's right," Jeremy murmured, holding his shoulder. "It only takes one."

* * *

Just as Harry emerged from the subway, on his way to
- the Center, a thunderstorm broke. Harry knew it would be over quickly, but meanwhile there were gusty winds and a driving rain. Harry rushed to a doorway for shelter. To his surprise, he found someone already there, his jacket collar up and his hands in his jacket
- pockets. It was Ben Beck.

Ben scowled as Harry joined him, but Harry suspected that Ben was more miserable than hostile. Harry didn't waste any words. "You almost clipped me with your car the other night. How come?"
- Ben didn't answer. He just shrugged and looked out into the rain.

They stood there silently. The rain began to get softer and lighter, until before long there were only a few drops coming down.

"Are you going right home after class tonight?" Harry wanted to know.

Ben simply said, "Nothing to go home for."

"We could stop somewhere for a beer," Harry said.

Ben said nothing, but he nodded his head to mean yes.

Chapter Thirteen

Linda Prime had been invited to a "sleepover" at the home of her friend, Dorothy. The last "sleepover" she'd been to was one in which the girls had stayed up virtually the whole night, with the result that they'd slept through the whole of the next day. Harry was tempted to put his foot down and refuse permission, but he didn't.

This enabled Tyrone to claim the right to invite some of *his* friends over. When he did, there flashed through both his mind and his father's the recollection of the pre-

- vious occasion on which Tyrone had had his friends over.

   Things hadn't gone well. It all started when Harry got a phone call that led to his having to be absent for an hour or two. Up until that time, the boys—Eddie, Len-
- nie and Max—hadn't exactly been enjoying themselves. Eddie had been examining Tyrone's monster models, and when Godzilla somehow collapsed, Tyrone suspected that Eddie had done something to it on purpose. Meanwhile, Lennie had secluded himself with the TV set
- in one corner of the room, and Max had the record player turned up high in the other corner, where he was listening to some of Tyrone's collection of old Beatle records. After a while, Tyrone and Eddie began swinging pillows at each other, half in fun and half in earnest.
- With the three cots arranged around Tyrone's bed, there was no room left on the floor, so they had to chase each other around on top of the cots and the bed.

   Eddie had put his glasses on a dresser, but he stumbled and fell right on the dresser top, smashing his glasses
- to bits. That annoyed him very much (he could just im-

agine what his father would say the next morning), so he brought his pillow down on Tyrone's head as hard as he could, but the pillow ripped and so, shortly after, did Tyrone's. Feathers filled the room, swirling about and rising up to the ceiling again as the boys seized new pillows and continued their battle. With all the feathers and noise, Lennie could hardly see or hear his program, but he kept watching unmoved. Just then Max, who was barefoot, cut his foot on a piece of glass and went hopping about the house, dripping drops of brilliant red blood on the toast-colored carpet. It was at this point that Harry returned. His only comment was, "You mean, the cat didn't throw up *too*?" Harry got Max's foot patched up, and eventually the boys got to bed. Finally, when everything seemed quiet, the cat threw up on the living room carpet.

So Tyrone firmly expected the answer to be "No!" But instead his father rather mildly inquired who would be invited. Tyrone had already decided that a change of guests would be advisable, so he said, "Steve and

Ramon and Dudley." To his amazement, his father said it would be all right.

It was a quiet evening, filled with good conversation. They talked about the motorcycles they would like to have, the movies they had seen and would like to see; they talked about teachers, about parents, about a whispered exchange between two girls that Steve had overheard, and about something one of Dudley's friends had secretly shown him. They exchanged exaggerations about their ability to drive, and they spent about a half hour discussing where babies come from.

"Well, you didn't just think they came out of nowhere, did you?" Steve demanded. "You can't get something out of nothing, you know!"

"Wait a minute," objected Tyrone. "Since you're so smart, tell me where the world came from!"

"It was made by God," Dudley said. "In the Bible it says that in the beginning God made heaven and earth."

"My teacher says the earth and the other planets were once part of the sun," Tyrone replied.

"But that's the earth," said Ramon, "not the universe. What we're talking about is, how did the universe begin."

"How do we know it began?" Steve asked. "How do we know it wasn't always there?"

"How could anything always be there? Everything has to have a beginning," Dudley insisted.

"The universe doesn't have to come to an end," said Steve, "so why couldn't someone say that it didn't have a beginning?"

Dudley shook his head. "How could the universe not have a beginning? I can imagine the universe without the earth, or without the sun. But I can't imagine there being no universe at all—just nothing. The universe is here, that's a fact. So it must have begun somehow. I just can't imagine it *not* beginning."

"And I can't imagine it *beginning*," Steve answered quickly. "So I guess it's unimaginable either way. But you don't prove anything at all when you say it's something you can imagine happening or can't imagine happening."

Dudley remarked, "Look, when I said before that everything has a beginning, what I meant was that everything has a *cause*. Everything happens because something else makes it happen. Someone applies a match to the gas, and that causes a fire in the stove. The fire causes the water to heat and form steam. The steam causes the whistle of the kettle to blow, and so on. Everything has a cause, and each thing is the cause of something else happening."

Later on, when they were all in their beds and the room was almost completely dark, Steve returned to the topic they had been discussing. "Dudley, you said everything has a cause," he said. "But you know, if all the *parts* of the universe were caused, that still wouldn't prove that the universe itself had a cause."

"I don't get you," Dudley said.

"Well, look," Steve tried to explain, "the parts of a machine could all be small, but that wouldn't necessarily mean that it was a small machine. The parts could be light, and still it could be a heavy machine. So what's true of the part doesn't have to be true of the whole. And so it could be that the parts of the world were all caused, but that doesn't mean that the world itself was caused."

Ramon put in, "So we're back to where we were before—you were saying that the universe may not have had a beginning."

"That's crazy!" said Dudley.

Steve sat up. "Look," he said, "there are two possibilities, right? Either the world had a beginning or it didn't, right?"

"Right," said Tyrone. "But there's another question here. That's the question of whether or not the world was created by God."

"The world just had to be created by God," said Dudley. "That's the only possibility."

Steve didn't hear Dudley's comment, because he had gotten out of bed and turned on the light. Tyrone had fallen asleep, but the light woke him up, and he pulled his pillow over his head. Steve produced a piece of paper, and said, "Let me show you guys something. My

- cousin—he's a mathematics teacher in high school—once showed it to me. If you've got a set of two things, say, ice cream and cake, each has two possibilities: either you've got ice cream or you don't.
- And, either you have cake or you don't. So now put the two sets together and that gives you four possibilities: first, ice cream and cake; second, cake but no ice cream; third, ice cream but no cake; and fourth, neither ice cream nor cake."
- "Hey, that's cool," said Dudley. "I can do that too. Franks and beans; franks but no beans; beans but no franks; and neither beans or franks."

From under the pillow came Tyrone's muffled voice: "Girls and boys; girls without boys; boys without girls;
- and no boys or girls at all. Now why don't you guys put out the light and let's get some sleep?"

Everyone said, "Shut up, Tyrone," but no one said anything else for a moment.

Then Ramon exclaimed, "Hey, Steve, I see what you
- were driving at! We were talking about whether the

world began, and whether there was a God, and you brought that up about four possibilities. So how would that work on what we were talking about?"

"Well, look," Steve replied, "it's easy:

First: The world had a beginning, and was created by God.

Second: The world had a beginning, but wasn't created by God.

Third: The world didn't have a beginning and was created by God.

Fourth: The world didn't have a beginning, and wasn't created by God."

"The third one isn't possible," said Dudley. "It contradicts itself. Only the first, second, and fourth ones are possible."

"Okay, maybe," said Steve. "But remember, I wasn't talking about what's *true*, I was just talking about what's possible. You may believe the world will end, but it's *possible* it won't. And you can believe it began if you want to, but it's *possible* it didn't."

Tyrone turned off the light again, and then, before he stretched out in bed, he said, half to himself and half to the other boys, "My father says you don't have to be always looking for answers. I mean, you can think about something without having to find out what the right answer is. There are lots of different ways of looking at things and of thinking about things. But I guess you have to find out about them for yourself. You get taught that there's only one way to think, and then you find out there are a lot of other ways that may be just as good. I'd like to find out all the different ways in which it's possible to think."

"And I'm interested," Steve responded, "in finding out the *right* way to think."

Ramon would have said, "So am I," but by that time he was half asleep.

As for Steve, once asleep he dreamt that he was in a great castle, looking down from a window on the cobblestoned courtyard. A large square had been marked off on the cobblestones, and that square was itself composed of four smaller squares. An old inn stood nearby with a creaking signboard that read, "The Four Possibilities." There was a girl in the courtyard playing hopscotch on the cobblestones. At first he couldn't see who it was. Then she turned around. It was Debra Gordon, looking incredibly beautiful. She was smiling and holding out the ball to him, only it wasn't a ball any longer; it was a tomato or apple or something, he couldn't tell what. All at once she disappeared, and he was running from third base during a sandlot game, trying to slide into home plate, and the catcher was a tall knight in armor. The knight lifted his helmet. It was his father. That was the end of his dream.

Chapter Fourteen

When Suki said she'd never visited the art museum, Anne proposed that they go together the following Sunday afternoon. Consequently, when Sunday arrived, they found themselves going from one handsome room to the next. Suki was amazed at the great tapestries, the thick carpets, the magnificent curving staircases. The paintings she found more difficult to enjoy. Anne would watch Suki's face intently as they passed from picture to picture, hoping that at some point it would show some sign of delight.

It wasn't that she *didn't* like the paintings, Suki tried to explain, but she couldn't honestly say that she did. But when she saw the painting of St. Francis coming out of his cave to enjoy the sun, Suki turned to Anne with a flashing smile, although she said nothing. And when she came upon the life-size sculpture of Diana, the huntress-goddess, slender and lovely and poised, Suki walked around and around it.

"How beautiful she looks without clothes," Suki said at last.

"And how awful she'd look if she had any on," Anne replied and the girls laughed together. But as they walked from the room, it was Anne who turned and looked steadfastly again for a long moment at Diana.

They turned into the peristyle of the museum—an inner courtyard roofed over with greenish glass. In the center of the pool was a graceful fountain in which bronze cherubs and dolphins played merrily together. And all around the pool were splendid shrubs and plants. A concert in one of the adjoining rooms could be overheard, although the girls had difficulty identifying the instruments. Anne said it was a violin, cello and piano. Suki thought it might be a harpsichord and two violas.

As they sat on the marble bench, Suki gazed about her with quiet pleasure. But Anne was angry at herself for having forgotten to bring her sketchbook. She would have liked to sketch Suki's face. Suki's face was so marvellously different! Every detail was so delicate and so perfect—her eyes, her cheekbones, her bangs—what a beautiful portrait could be made of them!

"I love these plants," said Suki. "I love all plants. At home I have a garden. I like to see things grow and bloom. And I like digging in the ground. It's funny, sometimes when I'm upset, I'll work in the garden, and I'll feel better afterwards."

"I didn't know you did that sort of thing," said Anne, to whom gardening was rather dirty and unnecessary work. "Why doesn't your husband take care of your garden?"

"Well, he did, when he had time, but he died last year."

"Oh!" said Anne. She was quite shocked. Then she remembered something. "But you have a child!"

"Yes," Suki replied with a little smile. "He'll soon be three years old."

Anne wasn't sure what to say. After a moment, she remarked, "I love flowers, too. Especially when they're freshly cut, and I can arrange them in a vase myself, and if I like them enough I sometimes paint them." She paused again, then asked, "Did you ever try writing about flowers?"

Suki laughed. "I tried a number of times, but it was pretty bad. They were very ordinary. But I did once write something about flowers that I still like. It had only five words:

> "Gardeners,"
>
> roses think,
>
> "never die."

Anne wasn't sure what the poem—if it *was* a poem—was all about, so she made no comment.

Suki traced her finger along the giant leaf of a philodendron. "I suppose I like cut flowers too," she said, "but they die, and I don't like to watch things die." Suddenly she remembered something, and her face lit up enchantingly. "Once we had a plant called a night-blooming cereus. Did you ever see one? They're tropical plants. They bloom only once in four years. The night it was about to bloom, we put spotlights around it, and had a big party with all our friends, and stayed up all night. And oh, the bloom was so beautiful! You should have seen it! It was something like a huge lily, but very deep inside. It was lovely!" Suki sighed, then she smiled as she caught sight of a cherub wrestling with a dolphin.

Anne smiled too, not at the cherub, but because it made her so happy to see Suki happy. "Oh, Suki," she exclaimed, "you've got to come to my home some time! We've got all sorts of interesting things there. My mother paints, and she has her paintings hanging all over the place, but you probably wouldn't like them. And my father has the most wonderful collections. You should see his butterfly collection. He's got them in glass cases, so carefully arranged and pinned—"

Suki tried not to shudder, but she couldn't help it, and Anne couldn't help seeing it. Anne reproached herself for not having realized that Suki couldn't stand to see things hurt. She couldn't even stand hearing about them being hurt.

Anne put her hand on Suki's for a moment. "Suki, I'm sorry. I suppose it *is* cruel, pinning butterflies, although my father does anesthetize them first. But I wish you would come home with me. My father and mother would love to meet you. They'd find you so *interesting!*"

"Like a butterfly?" Suki asked, and instantly she could have bit her tongue, she was so sorry she had said it. It was a cruel thing to have said, Suki thought, and Anne had meant no harm. As for Anne, her eyes filled with tears and her face was flushed.

"No, Suki, no, no, it's nothing like that!" was all that Anne could say. She didn't think Suki's remark was cruel, because she thought she'd somehow deserved it. "Suki thinks of herself as a perfectly ordinary person," Anne reflected, "so I guess when I said my parents would find her interesting, she must have thought I was treating her like some kind of freak! And maybe I was. After all, when she and her husband had all those friends in to see that night-blooming plant, there wasn't anything wrong with that, because a plant is just a thing. But Suki's a person, and you don't treat a person like a thing, no matter who it is! And that's what I was doing. It's like I was *using* her, the way I use the cut flowers when I arrange them to make a still life. Oh, I feel awful!"

Then Anne found Suki tugging gently at the puff of her sleeve. "It's all right, Anne," Suki said gently, "it's all right. I shouldn't have said that, and I'd love to come visit you."

As they traced their way back through the rooms of

the museum, Suki stopped in front of a portrait. "He's pretty, isn't he?" she said with a smile.

"That's Titus," replied Anne. "He was Rembrandt's son. I believe he was about eight years old when this was painted, but I think he died a while later."

Suki was no longer smiling. "Poor man," she said, "it's hard to lose someone you love very much."

As they walked home through the park, Anne said, "It's funny, to me that was always just a nice painting. But to you, it was like it was a real person."

"Oh, no," replied Suki, "I know the painting wasn't a real person. In fact, I guess that's why I've never liked paintings much, because they're not alive. I really like it when you point out the colors to me and how they're arranged, but to me, paintings have always been just big smeary squares of canvas. It's only when it's got something to do with life or with people that I can find any interest in it." Suki smiled when she saw Anne frown at her remarks. "After all," she concluded, "people and things are very different, and to me a painting is just a thing."

"But you like plants," protested Anne, "and plants are just things."

"Well, but they're living things," Suki countered.

"Maybe they're living," said Anne, "but they've got no feelings, and they don't show any kind of expression. And yet paintings, even though they're just things, *do* show expression. So it's not as simple as you thought." To herself, Anne added, "It's not as simple as *I* thought, either."

Suki said softly, "I've always thought of paintings as just pretty things, like bracelets—you know, something ornamental. I never thought of them as having feelings."

"Well, they don't *have* them," replied Anne, "but they do *show* them. And not only feelings, but ideas, too. Lots of times I can just look at a painting and it's as if I knew right away what the painter's thought was."

Suki considered what Anne said, then she responded, "So plants are part of nature and don't show feelings. And paintings are man-made, and they do show feelings. But what about the human face and the human body? They're not man-made, and yet they do show feelings. So that's a third type altogether, isn't it?"

Anne put her arm around Suki's shoulder and gave her a little hug, and though she didn't say a word, she smiled as if to say, "Yes, Suki, that's it, yes...yes...yes."

* * *

The same Sunday Lisa and Fran went to the movies together. Fran didn't live far from the theatre, so that afterwards Lisa agreed to stop in at Fran's for a while before going home.

"How many brothers do you have, Fran?" Lisa asked, looking at some snapshots on the dresser.

"Three," said Fran, smiling, "all younger than me."

"That's funny," said Lisa, "I have three brothers, too, but they're all older than me—lots older. I'm the youngest. But they're nice, my brothers, even though they still tease me a lot. When they start teasing me, I think I could murder them. I could just strangle them." She laughed as she said it, and Fran knew she really didn't mean it. "None of my brothers went to college," Lisa continued. After a moment, she added, "How about yours?"

"None of us did," Fran replied quietly. "I wanted to be a lawyer."

"Why a lawyer?" Lisa asked.

"Because I think lawyers can do the most for Black people," Fran answered. "It's as simple as that."

Lisa picked up a little wooden carving. "This is nice," she remarked. "Where did it come from?"

"From Tanzania," said Fran. "One of my brothers visited there once and brought it back with him. I'd love to go there some day."

"Life must be hard there," Lisa commented.

"Well, they're poor, yes," Fran replied quickly, "and they don't have all sorts of things that we have here. But if you mean are they a bunch of savages, I'd say no. Let me tell you something," Fran went on, her eyes flashing. "Over here, in this country, no matter how good times are, there are always lots of people who are starving, and no matter how bad things get, there are lots of people who have plenty. But my brother told me in parts of Africa, it's not like that. Over there, when there's starvation, no one has plenty, and when there's plenty, no one starves. So what I want to know is, who're the savages, them or us?" Fran relaxed a bit and remarked, "Anyway, that's how it *was*. Whether it still *is* that way, I don't know."

Lisa said nothing. She was very much impressed with how strongly Fran seemed to feel about some things. Lisa would have liked Fran to talk some more about herself and what she believed, but suddenly Fran was her old self again and seemed unwilling to talk about anything that might be personal. It occurred to Lisa that it must have been rare for Fran to invite someone whom she was not very familiar with, just as it was rare for Fran to discuss her thoughts about herself with anyone. Lisa had no wish to invade Fran's privacy, and she decided to change the subject.

"Fran," she said, "tell me, what do you think of what Harry and Tony are doing?"

"You mean turning sentences around, and asking what follows from what, and always asking for reasons whenever anyone says something, and always wondering how to explain things that happen?" Fran replied.

Lisa nodded. "That's right," she said, tossing her long hair back over her shoulders. "Harry's very excited about it, and he works hard on it, and lots of times he doesn't get anywhere and he knows it. But Tony thinks everything's very simple. Like he has one number, he adds a second to it, and then he figures out what the third one is—it's the sum of the first two—you know, like seven plus three make ten. So he thinks that if you take one sentence, and you add another one to it, you should be able to get a third sentence which is the result of adding the first two together."

Fran laughed. "I think it annoys you a little that Tony is right so often," she remarked, "but in this case, he is right, isn't he?"

"I'm not sure he is, Lisa said. She had picked up a pencil and a yellow note pad from Fran's desk, and had been doodling on it. But now she wrote down one of the examples that she and Harry and Tony had talked about a few days before.

All dogs are animals.

<u>All collies are dogs.</u>

Therefore: All collies are animals.

"See," she said, pointing with her pencil to the first two lines, "it's just like Tony said. If you're given the first two sentences, you can figure out the third, just like adding two numbers together and getting their sum."

Fran studied the example for a few moments and then commented, "No, Lisa, it's not quite the same. Because a sum is *equal to* the two numbers you've added. But what you have here is a conclusion that you've drawn from the two sentences you started with. And the conclusion isn't at all the same as those two starting sentences."

Lisa frowned. "Why not?" she wanted to know.

"Because, look," Fran pointed out, "you had the word 'dogs' in your first sentence, and you had it again in your second sentence, but in your third sentence, it's missing completely!"

"That's right," Lisa exclaimed, "it drops out!" She bit the rubber eraser on the pencil for a moment and then she said, "Let's try another example and see if the same thing happens." On the yellow pad, she wrote:

All stores are businesses.

<u>All supermarkets are stores.</u>

Therefore: All supermarkets are businesses.

"You see," said Fran, triumphantly, "the word 'stores' appears in each of the first two sentences, but that seems to cancel it out. The other words, 'businesses' and 'supermarkets,' appear only once in the first two sentences, but then they show up again in the conclusion."

"There's something else I notice," Lisa said. "In the first sentence, the word 'stores' is in the beginning, but in the second sentence, it's at the end. I wonder if that makes a difference."

Fran quickly saw the point. "There's only one thing to do," she asserted. "We've got to see if it still works changed around some other way. Let's see now . . ." and for a moment she buried her face in her hands and concentrated. Then suddenly she threw her hands apart, and with a flashing smile she said, "I've got it! How about this." Taking the pencil and pad from Lisa, she wrote:

All chairs are furniture.

<u>All tables are furniture.</u>

Therefore: All chairs are tables.

Lisa looked at Fran with a startled expression. "It didn't work!" she exclaimed. "Chairs aren't tables. It must be that when you put the word 'furniture'—the word that cancels out—*at the end* of each of the first two sentences, you made the conclusion turn out false!"

"Hey!" Fran said enthusiastically, "I think we found out something that Tony and Harry have been looking

—168—

for all along and couldn't find—the secret of why some pairs of sentences produce a true conclusion, and some produce a false conclusion."

"Wait," said Lisa, who was just as excited as Fran, "let me try one more example."

<u>All eyes are parts of the body.
All eyes are things that see.</u>

Therefore: All parts of the body are things that see.

Fran clapped her hands together. "Oh, Lisa, look! You put the word that cancels out—'eyes'—*in the beginning* and again that made the conclusion false!"

Lisa replied, "Fran, I don't think we can say for sure yet that what we've done is right. There may be cases like the one I gave you before where the conclusion turns out true instead of false. Maybe we just haven't tried enough different types yet and maybe there are some rules we don't know yet."

Not many days later, Lisa got on the bus in the morning to go shopping, and to her delight found Fran on the same bus. The two of them chatted together for a few minutes. Then they became aware that the two men sitting in the seat in front of them were talking rather loudly, and seemed angry about something. They overheard one of the men say, "This country is really going to the dogs. And it's all because of these people who're always agitating for their civil rights. Every time I look in the paper, I read about some lawyer defending some radical. Did you ever notice how all the lawyers in this country are in favor of civil rights? And did you ever notice how all the radicals in this country are in favor of civil rights? So what more proof do you need that all lawyers are radicals?"

Fran quickly wrote on the back of an envelope:

        All lawyers are people who favor civil rights.

        <u>All radicals are people who favor civil rights.</u>

Therefore: All lawyers are radicals.

And underneath, Fran wrote the example which she had used the other day:

All chairs are furniture.

<u>All tables are furniture.</u>

Therefore: All chairs are tables.

She showed the envelope to Lisa and Lisa squealed with delight: "I know, I know—I noticed the same thing. It didn't follow then that 'all chairs are tables,' and it doesn't follow here that 'all lawyers are radicals.' "

The bus stopped in front of the department store and they both got out. Fran smiled and said, "At least there's one thing I learned."

"What's that?" Lisa asked.

"The sort of things that would have been said about me if I ever got to be a lawyer," Fran replied.

Chapter Fifteen

Linda was writing something at her desk when Harry put his hand through the doorway and asked, "You guys want to take a walk? I have to get a pack of cigarettes."

"Tyrone's out with Steve," said Linda. "But I'll go with you."

"He's sure in a hurry to get those cigarettes," Linda thought to herself as her father walked briskly along. She deliberately slowed her pace down a bit. "Dad," she said, "why do you smoke?"

"Because I like to," Harry replied.

"But they say that smoking causes cancer," Linda insisted.

Harry said, "Only if you smoke too much."

"I don't see how you can be sure when it's not too much and when it is," Linda remarked. "Besides, I've tried your cigarettes and they taste awful."

"That's good!" said Harry, amused at her confession. "Maybe you won't pick up the habit that way."

After a few moments, Linda asked, "Did cigarettes taste awful to you when you first tried them?"

"I don't remember. It was a long time ago. It seems to me I didn't like their taste much at first, but then I kept on smoking and pretty soon I began to like it."

"How long ago was it?" Linda wanted to know. "When you were in high school?"

Linda's father laughed. "No, I was a slow starter. It was when I was in the Army."

"I have a teacher who was in Viet Nam," Linda said slowly. Harry gave her a puzzled glance. He was unsure where the conversation was going.

There was another pause. Then Linda asked, "Dad, how do wars start?"

"Oh, you know how it is," said Harry. "People hate each other and the first thing you know, they're fighting."

"Is that how it was with the Viet Nam war?" Linda asked, with a frown.

Harry shook his head. "Come to think of it, it was just the opposite. The people on both sides didn't dislike each other until they began fighting."

"So how come?" Linda demanded. "First you tell me one thing and then you tell me another."

"I don't know how come," Harry answered. "I never really thought of it."

They stopped at a street corner and waited for the traffic light to change. They were in sight of the drug store where Harry would get his cigarettes. But Linda was in no hurry. "So, Dad," she said, "first you smoked and you didn't like it but you *got* to like it. And first people fought, and as they did so, they *got* to hate each other."

Harry hurried into the store, bought his cigarettes, opened the pack, removed a cigarette and began to smoke. "So why am I being cross-examined today?" he wanted to know. "You want me to take up bubble gum, is that it?"

Linda grinned. "Well, I just couldn't let you get away with saying that you smoked 'because you liked to.' You never let *me* get away with an answer like that!"

* * *

A few evenings earlier, someone had used the expression in class, "Water seeks its own level." Kevin had let it pass at the time, but this evening he had come prepared. He had brought along a U-shaped glass tube and a bottle of water. He poured the water in one side of the U-tube, and after bouncing up and down a moment, the water settled down to being the same level on both sides of the tube.

"Now you see," said Kevin, "many, years ago, people were quite superstitious, and they thought that water was like a living thing. When they would see water from mountain springs run down to the sea, or when they would watch rain water flatten out on the ground, they would say, 'Water seeks its own level.' But of course, that was wrong. The water wasn't *trying* to find its own level, was it? It doesn't have a mind. It's just a thing, just a physical object. So in the U-tube here, where the two sides finally become even, it isn't because 'Water seeks its own level,' as people used to say. It's just that water obeys the law of gravity.''

Tony's hand shot up. "Kevin, wouldn't water have to have a mind in order to do what you said, 'obey the law of gravity'?"

Kevin grinned and shook his head. "Tony, you're absolutely right! That was a foolish thing for me to have said, and I'm not laughing at you, I'm laughing at myself. Of course water doesn't *obey* the law of gravity, the way a person obeys a traffic light. The law of gravity doesn't tell things how they *ought* to behave; it just describes how they *do* behave. So it's silly for me, or for anyone, to say, 'Water obeys the law of gravity.' "

Some of the members of the class saw the point and were amused along with Kevin and Tony. But others didn't get it, and there wasn't time to continue the discussion. The next evening, however, Kevin showed the U-tube experiment again and explained again about the law of gravity. Then he somehow got on the subject of rocks, and he passed samples of different kinds of rocks around the class. Tom Schultz held up one piece which sparkled in the light, and asked what it was.

"That's mica," said Kevin. "Look, you can chip off little fragments of it with your fingers."

"How come you can see through it?" asked Mike, who had taken the piece from Kevin and was squinting at it with one eye.

"Well," said Kevin. "It's transparent. Or almost transparent."

Hesitantly, Harry raised his hand. "Kevin," he said, "maybe it's a kind of stupid question to ask, but when

Mike just now wanted to know how come you could see through the mica, you said because it was transparent. So my question is, can we see through it because it's transparent, or is it transparent because we can see through it?"

"Ah, that's a good question, Harry," said Kevin, scratching his head a bit. "Look, if we can see through something, we may *describe* that thing as 'transparent.' But to understand how it happens that we see through it would require an *explanation.* So see, the word 'transparency' is just a name by which we describe a certain kind of behavior, but it doesn't *explain* anything."

"I can give you another example," Tony said to Harry. "If we were down on the Gulf of Mexico and the wind was blowing 200 miles an hour, and somebody said to me, 'Hey, Tony, why's the wind blowing 200 miles an hour?' and I said, 'Because it's a hurricane,' then that wouldn't be an answer, because I'd just have given a *name* to what was happening. I wouldn't have explained it in terms of what we know about the causes

- of hurricanes."

"Right," said Fran Wood. "Like if I asked you why someone I know hated certain types of people, and you said, 'Because he's a racist,' that wouldn't be an ex-
- planation, because 'racist' is just the concept we use to classify people who think and act in certain ways. It isn't the *cause* of their being that way."

"I've got another example," said Rudy Garlock. "If I stretch a rubber band and it snaps back, I call it
- 'elastic.' But it doesn't snap back *because* it's called elastic. It's just that it's classified as elastic because it's one of those things that snap back."

"And sugar doesn't dissolve because it's soluble," said Lisa. "It's just that it's called 'soluble' in view of
- the fact that it dissolves."

"How about this one?" said Jennifer Starr. "People don't fight all the time because they're 'combative.' It's just that 'combative' is a word to describe or classify people who're ready to fight all the time. It isn't the
- *cause* of their fighting; it's just a description."

At this, Harry shook his head and said, almost as if he were talking to himself, "I don't know, Jennifer. Sure, the word 'combative' isn't a cause of their fighting, but their readiness to fight certainly contributes to their fighting. If some people are always disposed to fighting, doesn't that help explain why they get in so many fights?"

Jennifer replied, but Harry didn't hear it, because his mind kept worrying over the distinction between *describing* and *explaining*. "Is it really so clear-cut?" he asked himself. "When we describe something, doesn't that description give directions to the way we will later explain it? And then when we do explain it, doesn't that affect the way we will describe it the next time?"

His mind gradually drifted away from the classroom conversation. He was reminded of the talk he had had with Linda. What was it about: do people fight each other because they're already mad at each other, or is their fighting the *cause* of their being mad at each other?

Harry thought too about their discussion of his smoking. "At first," Harry mused, "I didn't smoke because I liked to. I smoked because I wanted to be like all the tough guys in the cigarette ads. But gradually I came to like it, and from then on, I smoked because I liked it.

"In the same way," Harry thought, "a soldier might find himself in the army and be forced to fight, even though he didn't hate the 'enemy.' But after a while, after he had been fighting long enough and seen enough horrible things happen, he might develop a hatred that would cause him to fight some more.

"So what starts out as the effect may wind up as the cause," Harry said to himself, "and what starts out as the cause may wind up as the effect."

Then suddenly, Harry felt quite annoyed with himself. "Linda asked me why I smoked, and I told her because I liked to. But my liking to wasn't the original *cause* of my smoking, and it's never been a good *reason* for my smoking. Just because someone likes to do something doesn't necessarily mean he has a good reason for doing it. Linda was asking me to *prove* to her why smoking is good, so she could have proven to me why it isn't. But I never gave her a chance."

With that thought, Harry felt a wave of weariness wash over him. Never before had the plight of the single parent seemed so difficult. "How can two kids who're about to become teen-agers be guided by a parent who's himself only halfway rational?" he reflected.

As he looked around the room, he noticed Lisa talking animatedly to Suki. "Why look further?" he asked himself. And then he added, to his own amusement, "What those two kids need are *two* halfway rational adults, not just one!"

He stationed himself strategically at the door so he could intercept Lisa as she was leaving and ask her for a date.

Chapter Sixteen

Both Tony Basilio and his wife had to leave early each morning to go to work. It was much too early for Peter to go to school when they left, so they would set the alarm clock for him, and he would get up and dress, eat his breakfast and make his lunch with no one else in the apartment. But his mother always worried that he would oversleep and as a result would be late to school. In fact, that's exactly what she would say to him every night before he went to sleep: "Remember, Peter, if you oversleep, you'll be late to school."

- That weekend, the Basilios took a long trip by bus to visit Peter's grandparents. They didn't get back until late Sunday night. It had been a difficult, tiring weekend, and Mrs. Basilio was particularly worried that
- Peter might not be able to wake up the next morning when his alarm went off. As usual, she told him, "If you oversleep, you'll be late to school." But this time he *did* oversleep. And he *was* late to school. That was Monday.
- Monday evening Mrs. Basilio repeated her usual warning to Peter about oversleeping. The next morning Peter got up promptly when the alarm rang. But he had forgotten to get his clothes ready the night before, and now he couldn't find his shirt. He looked desperately
- through his dresser drawers. There wasn't a single shirt to be found. Finally, he decided to wait until his mother arrived at work. He then called her, and she told him to look among his father's shirts. He did and found that his shirts had been mixed in with his father's, but by the
- time he got dressed, he was late to school. That was

Tuesday.

On Wednesday, he was late once again, because he stopped to watch some firemen rescue a little boy from a house that was on fire.

It was very unusual for Peter to be late at all, not to mention being late three times in one week. He didn't like being late.

Besides, Peter kept a diary in which he noted things that happened to him. And something puzzled him. His mother always warned him, "If you oversleep, you'll be late." Well, what happened on Monday proved that she was right, because on Monday he'd overslept, and as a result he was late.

But what about Tuesday? He didn't oversleep on Tuesday or Wednesday and he was late anyhow on both those days.

Peter was tempted to forget it, but he couldn't get it out of his mind. He had a hunch that some kind of rule was there, just waiting to be discovered—a rule that would help him to figure things out. But he didn't know what it was. So he decided to talk to his father and mother about it.

Tony immediately got down to business. "Look, Peter," he pointed out, "what your mother said—it has two parts to it. The first part is '*if* you oversleep,' and the second part is 'then you'll be late'."

Adele Basilio couldn't restrain herself. "And Peter, don't you see," she said, "each of those parts can be either true or false! I mean, either you do oversleep, or you don't. And either you're late or you aren't."

"Right!" exclaimed Tony. "Adele, you've really got something there! Because now, don't you see, we can take what you told Peter, and we can ask what happens if the first part is true? Or, what happens if the first part is false? Or, what happens if the second part is true? Or, what happens if the second part is false? Don't you see, it's like the 'four possibilities' again."

Tony found a piece of scrap paper and began writing on it:

Monday   "If you oversleep, you'll be late."

First part true: <u>I overslept.</u>

Result: I was late. (It follows.)

Tuesday   "If you oversleep, you'll be late."

First part false: <u>I didn't oversleep.</u>

(What follows?)

Wednesday   "If you oversleep, you'll be late."

Second part true: <u>I was late.</u>

(What follows?)

Thursday   "If you oversleep, you'll be late."

Second part false: <u>I wasn't late.</u>

(What follows?)

The following evening, Tony showed Harry, Lisa and Fran what he and his wife and his son Peter had figured out. He copied on the blackboard what he'd written down on the piece of scrap paper.

- "I don't understand," said Fran. "What are you trying to do?"

"He's trying to see what follows from what," said Harry. "Look, it's easy to see in the case of Monday.
- Peter was told that if he overslept, he'd be late. Monday he did oversleep. So it follows that he would be late. And he was."

"Trouble is," said Lisa, "what about the other three days?"
- "Well," said Harry, "in the case of Tuesday, Peter didn't oversleep. But the first sentence talks about what happens only if you *do* oversleep. So the second sentence really has nothing to do with the first, and nothing follows."
- "That's just what *did* happen," said Tony. He didn't feel like saying Peter was late because he couldn't find a shirt to put on. "So okay, let's say that, where the first part is false, nothing follows."

"In that case," said Fran, "the same thing is true
- regarding Wednesday. If all you know is that someone

—190—

was late, you really can't tell if it was because he overslept, or because of something else that happened to him."

"So let's put down, where the second part is true, nothing follows," said Tony.

"But what about Thursday?" asked Harry. "Suppose all you know is that the second part was false. Does it tell you anything about the first part?"

"It has to," replied Fran. "If Peter got to school on time Thursday, that means he couldn't have overslept."

"That's right," said Tony, "He didn't."

"You know what that means?" exclaimed Harry, "that means if the second part is false, then the first part is false, too!"

From the back of the room, Kevin's voice could be heard saying, "Beautiful—just beautiful." He'd been sitting there on one of the desks, and they were so busy writing on the blackboard, they'd never noticed him. "Would you like me to summarize for you what you've done?" he asked.

"Please do," Fran said. The others just nodded.

"Well," said Kevin, "it seems to me you've discovered a wonderful rule that will work for any compound sentence beginning with the word 'if,' and assumed to be true. Remember, we assume the big sentence to be true, but we don't know whether the little sentences it contains are true or false. Now, the reasoning rule you've figured out works either when the first little statement is true or when the second little statement is false. If you find out that the first little statement is in fact true, it will follow that the second is also true. Or if you learn that the second little statement is in fact false, then the first one will also have to be false."

"Can you give us an example?" asked Lisa.

"Sure," said Kevin. "Assume this sentence to be true: 'If you're vaccinated, you won't get smallpox.' Now suppose I tell you that Harry here was vaccinated. On the basis of that one fact, what could you figure out all by yourself?"

"That's easy," Lisa laughed. "That Harry won't get smallpox."

"And now," said Kevin, "one other case. But this one is harder. Suppose I tell you that someone I know has just contracted smallpox. What could you figure out from that?"

"I don't know," said Lisa. "I give up."

"I know," Fran responded. "What follows is that the person you're speaking of must not have been vaccinated."

"Right," said Kevin. He turned to the board and wrote:

Assumed to be true:

    If he's vaccinated, he won't get smallpox.

Second part discovered to be false: He got smallpox.

Therefore, first part must be false:

    He hadn't been vaccinated.

Tony grinned. He would have a lot to tell his wife and Peter when he got home.

* * *

The TALE center that week proudly announced its latest expansion: a small room which could serve as a library and reading room. For those who could come to class early in the evening, or for those who were out of work, the library was a welcome and unexpected delight. Yet, on the very second evening after the opening of the library, Jennifer Starr caused consternation among the readers by loudly announcing that her wallet was missing and that she suspected Sam da Silva of taking it. Sam, just as loudly, denied the accusation.

A few minutes later, Rudy, who had gone down the hall to get a drink of water, noticed something wedged between the water fountain and the wall. It turned out to be Jennifer's wallet, and the contents, she agreed upon examining it, were intact. She did not, however, take back her accusation of Sam, and she developed an elaborate theory of why and how he had done it. She said Sam was the only person with the motivation to steal the wallet, because he had been saying earlier how badly he needed money.

"Jennifer," said Harry, "when was the last time you remember having your wallet before it was stolen, or whatever it was that happened to it?"

"Six o'clock," said Jennifer emphatically. Her face was still flushed and angry.

"Okay," said Harry, "and we found it at six forty-five. Whoever put it by the water fountain had to leave this room. But I can tell you that I was in this room from six to six forty-five, and Sam was, too. He never got up to go out."

Quickly, Tony wrote on the blackboard:

Assumed to be true: If Sam had taken the wallet,

        it would have been here in the room at 6:45.

Discovered to be true: It wasn't in the room at 6:45.

It follows that the first part must be false:

        Sam didn't take the wallet.

Fran commented, "It follows he didn't go out in the hall and hide it. It doesn't follow that he didn't take it."

But then Lisa had an idea. "You know what I think? I think Mike took the wallet."

- Kevin, who had been watching with his arms folded, remarked, "Lisa, all of these accusations! First Jennifer and now you! Accusations are serious! Do you have any evidence for what you're saying?"
- "Well," Lisa said, with a little laugh, "wouldn't it be just like Mike to do something like that? He's always playing practical jokes, and he likes to tease people—particularly Jennifer. Then too, that business of hiding it behind the water fountain. That's just the sort of
- thing Mike would do."

"You know what, Lisa," said Tony, "you know what it seems to me you're saying? You're saying this:

Assumed to be true: If Mike had taken the wallet, it would have been hidden behind the water fountain.

- *Discovered to be true:* It *was* behind the water fountain.

Conclusion that follows: Nothing.

"This is what we already agreed to, Lisa. If the second sentence is true, then nothing follows about the first little sentence. You've no proof against Mike at
- all!"

Just then, Sam rushed into the room, pulling Mike by the wrist. "Okay, Mike," Sam was saying angrily, "tell them what happened!"

"It was just a practical joke I was trying to play on Jennifer, honest," Mike whimpered. "I got sore at her because she always makes fun of me when I don't know the answer. But I didn't mean her any harm!"

"Well, you let Sam get blamed for it," said Kevin. "I don't think that's fair to Sam. What about you?"

Mike shook his head and looked at the floor. Then he and Kevin walked out of the room together, with Kevin doing most of the talking.

"Well," Lisa remarked a bit later, "I was right, wasn't I? I said it was Mike and it was!"

Fran and Harry looked at each other, but said nothing. Tony, however, couldn't help saying, "Lisa, you were right, but for the wrong reason. You just made a lucky guess, that's all. But you couldn't prove it."

Lisa laughed and her eyes twinkled mischievously. "Sure," she said, "I'll admit it. I couldn't have proved

- what I said. But I had a feeling, you know what I mean: a kind of hunch. And my hunch turned out to be right. After all, that's what's important, isn't it?"

- Kevin had returned in time to overhear Lisa's remarks. He said to her, "Yes, Lisa, you made a shrewd guess. And as it happened, you were right. But if you'd been wrong, another innocent person, like Sam, would have suffered. Guessing isn't a substitute for careful investigation, although it has its place. What I don't like,

- however, is making a reckless accusation about anyone just because you have a whim to do so."

  Harry could tell that Kevin's criticism had stung Lisa. Her face turned red and there were tears in her eyes. They sat together later that evening, after everyone else

- had left, talking about what had happened. Lisa was dejected now, and Harry wanted to try to cheer her up. He told her some amusing incidents about himself, and some other incidents in which Linda and Tyrone figured. He even got a little smile out of her.

- Then Harry remembered that he had resolved to ask

her for a date the other evening, but at the last moment, he had failed to summon up the courage to do so. This time he succeeded in asking her, only to be stunned by her reply.

"Harry," she said, "if you're interested in me because you're interested in *me*, okay. But if you're interested in me because you're thinking about your kids, well, I don't think so. I've got my own problems; I don't need yours. So if you don't mind, I'll just take a rain check."

With that she left. Harry stared at the blackboard in the empty room. Her reply had forced him to realize that it was *their* relationship that he was most interested in, and that she was the one he most wanted to be with.

Chapter Seventeen

With the holiday season approaching, Harry thought it might be a good idea to get some assurances from Kevin. "Kevin," he began, uncertain how to proceed, "I don't know how the others here feel about it, but speaking just for myself, I want to thank you for going along with us whenever we wanted to talk about reasoning and all that."

"It's no inconvenience to me," Kevin replied. "I can go with it either way."

Harry had hoped for a more positive response from

- Kevin, but he proceeded anyhow: "Well, I just wanted to know if, after the holidays, we could keep on bringing these things up, so that we can talk about them."

Kevin shrugged. "I have no objection. But how about
- the rest of you?"

Tony said, "Sure, let's keep on," and Mark and Fran nodded agreement.

But Lisa raised her hand, and Kevin called on her. "I think we've played around long enough with these silly
- rules," said Lisa. "I came here to brush up on my reading and writing and math skills, and I think that's what we should be doing more of from now on. If Harry and Tony want to talk about that other stuff, they can do it on their own. They're really the only ones who're in-
- terested in it, anyhow."

Harry was so surprised by Lisa's remarks that he could hardly find anything to say, and since Tony didn't think anything Lisa said was important enough to answer, he didn't reply to her either.

- So it was left for Fran to say, "But Lisa, I don't

understand you. For a long time you seemed to be very much interested in talking about how we think and thinking better and all that. So how come you're against it now?"

"Yeah," said Mark, "how come?"

"Well," Lisa began doubtfully, "it's not that I'm *against* it. I just wonder if it's worthwhile, or if it's really just a waste of time."

Kevin had thought at first that Lisa might not be serious, but now he realized she was. "You mean, you don't think you learned anything, Lisa?" he inquired.

Lisa pursed her lips for a moment, and then she observed, "Let me just say that I don't think I learned anything I didn't already know."

"Well, if you already knew it, you *couldn't* have just learned it," Maria Atley put in.

Lisa glanced at her quickly and said, "Obviously."

Harry was still trying to understand what was happening. He couldn't believe that Lisa would suddenly want to give up, just like that, because she didn't think

- they were getting anywhere. Was she annoyed because Kevin had criticized her for accusing Mike Morawski without evidence? Or was this her way of showing how offended she was when he asked her out?
- But now several other members of the class were beginning to say that they agreed with Lisa. Harry knew that if he didn't speak up now, the whole thing would be dropped. There would be no more class discussions about ideas and thinking and what was important and
- what wasn't important, such as he'd enjoyed so much in the past few months. He felt the class was looking at him, so he raised his hand, although he didn't know what he was going to say. He couldn't face the class; he turned to Kevin.
- "Kevin," said Harry, "I guess in a way Lisa's right. I guess different people understand things in different ways. Maybe something that seems clear to her doesn't seem clear to me, so I have to figure it out, and she thinks I should have known it all along. I don't know
- what else to say."

Harry had hoped he might be able to say something very clever, and he was disappointed in himself. Also, he felt he had let the others down too. Like Mark and Tony and Fran. Even though he knew he couldn't count on them to say anything, he also knew they counted on him.

Suddenly, Mike Morawski commented, "I don't know about anybody else, but I thought I learned something. Like I learned which sentences contradict which, and that's something we were never taught in English."

And Laura O'Reilly said, "And I still remember about how you can't turn a sentence around that begins with the word 'all,' like the other day when Rudy said to me, 'All girls are jerks,' and I said to him, 'Well, maybe so, but it doesn't follow that all jerks are girls, because I know at least one who isn't!' "

The class laughed, Rudy included.

Lisa raised her hand. Half under her breath, Tony said, "Aw, Lisa, what is it now?"

Kevin frowned at Tony and called on Lisa. "I've been

thinking over what Harry said," she remarked. "He said we each learn differently. Maybe he's right. People say I jump to conclusions all the time, and maybe that's what I was doing again. Anyhow, I didn't mean that we shouldn't talk in class about things we think are really important."

"I'm glad you're finally getting around to admitting it, Lisa," said Tony sarcastically. "Because you know darn well that what's true is true, and if it's worthwhile finding out about, we should find out about it."

"What's true is true," Lisa repeated coolly. "What are you going to tell us next, Tony, that cows are cows? Or that 2 equals 2?"

Kevin was about to rap on the desk for order when Harry indicated he wanted to say something again.

"You know," said Harry, "I can't help noticing something. Tony and Lisa aren't really disagreeing about what's true and what's not true. It's just that Tony is used to finding things out step by step, according to rules, the way we do mathematics, while Lisa seems to size things up very fast, like she'll have a hunch or something, and right away she has the answer. They simply have different methods of finding out."

"That doesn't prove his way is any better than mine," said Lisa.

"He can show how he proceeds, and you can't," said Maria.

"What makes you think I can't?" Lisa answered.

Now Kevin did rap on the desk. There was silence in the room for a moment, then Fran spoke up.

"It seems to me," said Fran, "that Tony and Lisa could both be right. I don't know quite how to say this because I haven't thought of it before. But I've been thinking, while I've been sitting here listening—I've been thinking of how all of us are here in one room. And it's the same room for all of us. And yet—" Fran stopped. "Oh, I don't know."

"Go on, Fran," Kevin said gently, "what is it you started to say?"

"I can't seem to express it," said Fran. "But you

know, here I am, sitting in the back of the room, and you're up there at the front of the room. And what do you see? You see faces. And what do I see? I see the backs of people's heads."

"And I'm sitting on the side of the room," exclaimed Anne, "and I see everyone from the side. I see their faces in profile."

"Well, that's what I mean," said Fran. "We're looking at exactly the same people in exactly the same room, and yet what we actually see is altogether different."

"So what you're saying," said Anne, "is that each of us is in the same world, yet we see things very differently. Oh, I know that's so true, because when my sister and I go to art class together, and even when we choose exactly the same still life to do, her paintings come out very different from mine. I think Fran's right. I think each of us lives in his own world that's different from other peoples'."

Now Harry was waving his hand wildly. Kevin nodded at him.

"Anne," said Harry, "I think you didn't interpret Fran correctly. I mean, I don't think that's what she was trying to say. Sure, from the back of the room, she sees a roomful of people with their backs turned to her, while Kevin sees only faces. But the important point is that, if she were to go up front, she would see only faces, and if Kevin were to go to the back of the room, he would see only backs of heads."

"Harry," said Lisa, "is all you're trying to say that we should try to see things from other people's points of view?"

Harry stared at Lisa blankly. Was that all he was trying to say? He wasn't sure, but there seemed to be more to it than that.

But Lisa went on without waiting for Harry's reply. "Well," she exclaimed, her eyes sparkling, "why doesn't anyone here try to understand *my* point of view? I disagree with you and right away everyone accuses me of copping out, or something like that!"

"Lisa," said Kevin, "I don't think anyone here called

you names or accused you of copping out. The trouble is, you've never really explained to us what you were objecting to. I wish you'd try to do so, just one more time. We'd like to be able to see things from your point of view, Lisa, but you haven't yet told us what it is."

"I don't think I can," Lisa said, trying to keep her voice steady, but not quite succeeding.

"Well, what started you thinking this way?" Kevin persisted in asking. "Was it something someone said here in class?"

Lisa shook her head. "No," she said, "no, it wasn't anything that anyone here said. It was something my father said to me. Well, it wasn't something he said, really, it was something he read."

"When was this?" asked Kevin.

"Oh, years and years ago." Lisa replied. "I'd been telling him how I was wondering about the mind and how it works, and he was very much interested. Then he got out a book that I'd often seen him read. It was a book of poetry, and he showed me a poem about the mind, but I couldn't understand it. It had a nice beginning: 'The mind is an enchanted thing,' or something like that, but all the rest of it was over my head. Then he showed me another, and even though it was also hard to understand, I thought it made more sense. It said the thoughts in our minds are like bats in a cave, and these ideas go flying about blindly, keeping within the walls. But then, in the last line, the poem says that every once in a while, 'a graceful error corrects the cave.' "

"What does *that* mean?" asked Melissa.

"That's what I asked my father," said Lisa, "and he tried to explain to me how something that seems to be a mistake may then turn out to be true, but this only happens if all of our knowledge is changed. Like he said, take Columbus. Everybody said that the world was flat, and that if Columbus kept on sailing he'd fall off the edge. They thought he was making a mistake. But afterwards they realized that if the world was understood to be round, it was no mistake at all."

"So what are you saying?" Tony asked. "That instead of learning how to think straight, we should learn how to make fancy mistakes?"

"I'm just saying," said Lisa patiently, "that you should keep an open mind, and don't think you know it all because you've figured out a few rules of thinking." Lisa looked for a moment more at Tony, and then glanced across the room at Harry. "I'd like to keep working on it, I really would. It was fun. And it does seem to work with the way we talk. But I don't think it works with the way we imagine, or the way we feel about things, or the way we dream . . ."

"I never said reasoning was just a matter of following some rules," Harry remarked, barely loudly enough for Lisa to hear him. But now the class was over, and people were beginning to stand up and collect their books and papers.

Lisa rose and stood before Harry. "I'm sorry I snapped at you the other day. If I wasn't sure why you wanted to take me out, I should have checked out the facts before jumping to conclusions. Another one of

Lisa Torrey's ill-founded accusations, I'm afraid. *My mistake. I'm sorry.*"

Harry looked at her intently. "No, you were right. The stuff about the kids *had* crossed my mind. But that's not where it stayed. I really would like to spend time with you. Are you interested?"

"I still have the raincheck," Lisa replied, with a smile. It was a tentative smile, but it was affirmative too.

"Sometimes a graceful error corrects the cave," Harry thought to himself. He liked the sound of it. He liked the idea of it. Once again, he said it to himself, "Sometimes a graceful error corrects the cave." He and Lisa walked together down the steps and out to the street while Kevin, standing in the doorway, kept watching them until they they were out of sight.